STILL AN OPEN DOOR?

THE AMERICAN UNIVERSITY PRESS PUBLIC POLICY SERIES

STILL AN OPEN DOOR?

U.S. Immigration Policy and the American Economy

Vernon M. Briggs, Jr.
and
Stephen Moore

The American University Press

Distributed by arrangement with
National Book Network
4720 Boston Way
Lanham, MD 20706

Library of Congress Cataloging-in-Publication Data

Briggs, Vernon M.
Still an open door? : U.S. immigration policy and the American
economy / Vernon M. Briggs, Jr. and Stephen Moore.
p.   cm. — (The American University Press public policy series)
Includes bibliographical references and index.
1. United States—Emigration and immigration—Economic aspects.
2. United States—Emigration and immigration—Government policy.
I. Moore, Stephen. II. Title. III. Series.
JV6471.B75   1994   330.973'092—dc20   94–19180 CIP

ISBN 1–879383–31–4 (cloth : alk. paper)
ISBN 1–879383–32–2 (pbk. : alk. paper)

 The paper used in this publication meets the minimum requirements of
American National Standard for Information Sciences—Permanence
of Paper for Printed Library Materials, ANSI Z39.48–1984.

Contents

Tables

Part Two: The Economic Case for More Immigrants

Stephen Moore

Preface

I mmigration is the third theme addressed by The American University Press
Public Policy series. The first two were abortion *(Abortion: Pro-Choice or
Pro-Life?* by Gary Crum and Thelma McCormack) and drugs *(Legalize It?* by
Arnold S. Trebach and James A. Inciardi). Like the topics of these earlier
volumes, immigration is subject to strong pro and anti analyses. Basically, this
volume poses two questions: Do immigrants hurt or help us economically? And,
have large numbers of immigrants enhanced our economic well-being or taken
jobs from American workers and lowered our standard of living, and will this
continue to be the case? Stephen Moore argues that immigrants always have
been, and will continue to be, good for our economy. Vernon Briggs warns that,
unlike in earlier times, immigrants arriving today have and will continue to have
adverse effects on our economy, mostly because our industrial and occupational
patterns have changed dramatically since the early part of the century.

Ever since the "new immigrants" began arriving in large numbers in the
1880s (non-English-speaking Catholics and Jews from Eastern and Southern
Europe), the United States has had an ambivalent relationship with immigrants.
On the one hand, we take pride and pleasure in describing ours as a country of
immigrants. On the other, we are fearful and skeptical that "these immigrants"
(meaning, any new arrivals from any country or region of the world) will hurt
us economically and socially: they will take jobs, lower our standard of living,
undermine our social and moral standards, and remain outside the mainstream
of American life. They will never assimilate.

Data from national random-sample polls demonstrate the strong anti-immigrant strain that has run through American society since at least the 1930s. For example, the following question has been asked on national polls since 1946: Should immigration be kept at its present level, increased, or decreased? Consistently over this period, less than 10 percent of the American public has favored increasing immigration levels. In the 1980s, 50 percent or more of respondents advocated decreasing the number of immigrants admitted to this country. In the 1970s, when large numbers of refugees were permitted entry (largely from Asia as a result of the Vietnam War), most Americans favored "keeping them out." Public opinion data also reveal a lack of support for amnesty for immigrants who have entered this country illegally, and strong support for banning employment of undocumented immigrants. Such attitudes exist side by side with the pride we Americans feel and express about our immigrant past and about the contributions made by earlier immigrants to our nation's well-being. Despite this pride, poll data and other indices of public opinion show that for more than a century, Americans have perceived their present-day immigrants as dangerous to our "way of life" and threatening to our economic well-being—regardless of where they come from and regardless of their characteristics.

In this debate, Vernon Briggs advocates stronger and more restrictive immigration policies, and a reassessment of the priorities established for admission of immigrants. He strongly urges "an employment-based admission system" over our current "family-reunification system." On the other side, Stephen Moore argues that immigrants bring much-needed "skills, talents, energies, and ambitions" to the United States, not only giving us a major competitive advantage economically, but also strengthening and rejuvenating our national spirit.

Like the drug and abortion debates in this series, both authors use empirical data (e.g., occupational and educational characteristics of recent and current immigrants) to bolster their analyses and support their positions. Reading this book may change your views about whether more immigrants are "good" or "bad" for the US economy.

RITA J. SIMON
Series Editor

About the Authors

Vernon M. Briggs, Jr. is a professor of labor economics in the New York State School of Industrial and Labor Relations at Cornell University. He has written widely on the subjects of labor, employment, and immigration, including: *Mass Immigration and the National Interest* (1992); *Labor Economics: Theory, Institutions, and Public Policy* (with Ray Marshall, 1989); *The Population and Labor Force of New York* (with Leon Bouvier, 1988); and *Immigration Policy and the American Labor Force* (1984). He holds an M.A. and Ph.D. from Michigan State University.

Stephen Moore is an economist at the Cato Institute, a Washington, DC-based think tank. He was previously a senior economist at the Joint Economic Committee as an assistant to Congressman Dick Armey of Texas. He also was the executive director of the American Immigration Institute, an organization dedicated to studying, promoting, and celebrating the impact of immigration on the United States. He is a regular contributor to the *Wall Street Journal, Human Events,* and *National Review,* and he has appeared on "MacNeil/ Lehrer News Hour," "Jesse Jackson Show," and news broadcasts of the CNN, NBC, and Fox networks. He is a graduate of the University of Illinois and completed his graduate work in economics at George Mason University.

Part One

The Imperative of Immigration Reform

The Case for an Employment-Based Immigration Policy

Vernon M. Briggs, Jr.

Introduction

1

A s at its dawn, the latter decades of the twentieth century in America have witnessed the phenomenon of mass immigration.[1] In between, roughly from the outbreak of World War I in Europe in 1914 to the implementation of the Immigration Act of 1965 in 1968, immigration was of declining significance to the economic well-being of the nation. Over those fifty-four years, the nation turned inward to find and to develop its labor force, and a long-delayed process was finally set in motion to include groups that had hitherto been marginalized. With the exception of the Depression years of the 1930s, the period from 1914 to 1968 was the most economically prosperous that the United States has ever experienced.

When mass immigration last flourished, at the onset of the twentieth century, the United States had yet to become an economic superpower. Although the industrialization process was well underway, its full dimensions were yet unrealized. Indeed, the assembly line—the quintessential symbol of US economic preeminence by mid-century—was not introduced until 1913, just as the era of mass immigration was coming to an end. Agriculture was still the predominant sector of the economy and provided most employment, although manufacturing was rapidly ascending. The occupational structure was overwhelmingly characterized by manual jobs that rewarded physical exertion.

[1] For a more complete discussion of the causes and effects of mass immigration in the United States, see Briggs 1992.

Moreover, industrial expansion was occurring behind a wall of highly protective tariffs—the highest the nation had known until that time. In terms of their human capital attributes, the immigrants of the early twentieth century resembled those of the preceding century. Most were unskilled, poorly educated, and non-English-speaking. Nonetheless, their human capital characteristics generally met the labor demands of the day.

Now, as the twentieth century comes to an end, US industrial and occupational patterns bear faint resemblance to those prevailing at the beginning of the century. In short, the nation's labor market is undergoing a radical transformation. New forces are restructuring the demand for labor, and these, in turn, are leading to unprecedented changes in employment patterns. The labor supply is growing rapidly while at the same time undergoing unparalleled compositional changes.

Most of the forces altering the demand for labor in the United States also affect the other industrialized nations. These forces are associated with the nature and pace of technological change, the reduction of international trade barriers, and shifts in consumer spending habits. However, one factor that greatly influences the demand for labor in the United States, and which does not affect the other major industrialized nations on the same scale, is the adjustment effects associated with the marked reductions in national defense expenditures following the end of the Cold War.

Collectively, the consequences of these influences are reshaping occupational, industrial, and geographic employment patterns in the United States. Employment is declining in most goods-producing industries and in many blue-collar occupations, while it is increasing in most service industries and in many white-collar occupations. Regional employment trends are extremely unbalanced, with growth generally stronger in urban than in rural areas, particularly in the Southeast and West, and generally weaker in the Midwest and Great Plains regions.

Future demand for labor lies primarily in service industries located in metropolitan areas, in occupations that stress cognitive abilities rather than physical strength and stamina. As Lester Thurow (1992) poignantly writes, "the skills of the labor force are going to be the key competitive weapon in the twenty-first Century . . . [for] skilled labor will be the arms and the legs that allow one to employ—to be the masters of—the new product and process technologies that are being generated" (p. 51). Conversely, the escalation in skill requirements leads to diminishing demand for unskilled labor. William Brock, who served as secretary of labor during the Reagan administration, warns, "the days of disguising functional illiteracy with a high paying assembly line job that simply requires a manual skill are soon to be over. The world of work is changing right under our feet" (Brock 1987, 8).

The forces being exerted on the supply of labor constitute a uniquely American experience, one not shared by the other industrialized countries. The US labor force grew at a record rate throughout the 1970s and 1980s, and while projections for the 1990s indicate some slowing in this rate, growth is expected to remain substantial. Therefore, there has been no shortage of labor per se that would have warranted the resumption of mass immigration witnessed since 1965.

Of even greater significance, however, are the changes in the actual composition of the US labor force: the rate of increase in the number of women and minorities entering the labor force has been and will continue to be greater than that of (non-Hispanic) white men. Women in general and minorities in particular (with the possible exception of Asian Americans) have had fewer opportunities to be trained, educated, or otherwise prepared to work in the occupations that are forecast to be in greatest demand in the coming decades. They are disproportionately concentrated in occupations and industries that are already in decline or are most vulnerable to decline in the near future. No other industrialized country faces comparable pressures to accommodate so many new job-seekers or such rapid changes in the gender and racial composition of its labor force.

It is against this backdrop—a transformation in both the demand and the supply components of the US labor market—that mass immigration resumed after 1965. Mass immigration was restarted with little public awareness and with only minimal public debate about the anticipated consequences. The level of immigration to the United St :s slowly began to rise in the late 1960s, accelerated in the 1970s, and soared in the 1980s to the highest level for any decade in US history (see table 1). As a consequence of significant statutory, judicial, and administrative actions taken during the 1980s, the phenomenon is now institutionalized and is a fact of life for the 1990s. The post–1965 wave of mass immigration, unlike earlier immigrant waves, therefore shows "no evidence of imminent decline" (Bouvier 1991b, 18).

In addition to the quantitative dimension—that is, the sheer numbers involved—an equally consequential aspect of this phenomenon pertains to the human capital characteristics of most immigrants now entering the United States legally and illegally. Most are unskilled, poorly educated, and do not speak English. As George Borjas (1990) notes in his assessment of the economic impact of the contemporary immigration experience, "the more recent immigrant waves have less schooling, lower earnings, lower labor force participation

Table 1. Annual Legal Immigration to the United States by Immigrant Category, 1965–1991[a]

	Total	Immediate Relatives[b]	Relative Preference[c]	Occupational Preference[d]	All Others
1965	296,697	32,714	13,082	4,986	245,915
1966	323,040	39,231	54,935	10,525	218,349
1967	361,972	46,903	79,671	25,365	210,033
1968	454,448	43,677	68,384	26,865	315,522
1969	358,579	60,016	92,458	31,763	174,342
1970	373,326	79,213	92,432	34,016	167,665
1971	370,478	80,845	82,191	34,563	172,879
1972	384,685	86,332	83,165	33,714	181,474
1973	400,063	100,953	92,054	26,797	180,289
1974	394,861	104,844	94,915	28,482	166,620
1975	386,194	91,504	95,945	29,334	169,411
1976-TQ[e]	103,676	27,895	28,382	5,621	41,778
1976	398,613	102,019	102,007	26,361	168,226
1977	462,315	105,957	117,649	21,616	217,093
1978	601,442	125,819	123,501	26,295	325,827
1979	460,348	138,178	213,729	37,709	70,732
1980	530,639	151,131	216,856	44,369	118,283
1981	596,600	152,359	226,576	44,311	173,354
1982	594,131	168,398	206,065	51,182	168,486
1983	559,763	177,792	213,488	55,468	113,015
1984	543,903	183,247	212,324	49,521	98,811
1985	570,009	204,368	213,257	50,895	101,489
1986	601,708	223,468	212,939	53,625	111,676
1987	601,516	218,575	211,809	53,873	117,259
1988	643,025	219,340	200,772	53,607	169,306
1989	1,090,924	217,514	217,092	52,775	603,543
1990	1,536,483	231,680	214,550	53,729	1,036,524
1991	1,827,167	237,103	216,088	54,949	1,319,027

Notes: a. The categories listed comprise the largest groups of immigrants. The figures are for fiscal years which, as of 1976, begin on 1 October. During this period, minor changes were made in the criteria of some immigrant classes making up these categories.

b. Spouses of citizens, children of citizens (unmarried and younger than age twenty-one), and parents of citizens age twenty-one or older.

c. This comprises the first, second, fourth, and fifth categories of the immigrant preference system. The first preference allows the entry of unmarried sons and daughters of US citizens (age twenty-one or older). The second preference covers spouses and unmarried sons and daughters of aliens lawfully admitted for permanent residence. The fourth preference allows for the entry of married sons and daughters of US citizens. The fifth preference deals with brothers and sisters of US citizens, provided such citizens are at least twenty-one years old.

d. This comprises the third and sixth categories of the immigrant preference system. The third preference allows for the admission of members of the professions and scientists or artists of exceptional ability. The sixth preference covers skilled or unskilled occupations for which labor is in short supply in the United States.

e. TQ = transitional quarter, when the US government shifted its fiscal year to end on 30 September rather than 30 June.

Source: US Immigration and Naturalization Service, Washington, DC.

and higher poverty rates than earlier waves had at similar stages of their assimilation into the country" (p. 20).[2] Nor should it be surprising that immigrants of this present era have been found to make greater use of welfare assistance than earlier waves of immigrants (Borjas 1990, chap. 9; see also Borjas and Trejo 1991). Thus, the mass immigration flow of this era is out of step with the emerging labor-market trends in the nation. The many new immigrants are adding to the pool of low-skilled workers and job-seekers, the very group that is experiencing the greatest difficulty adjusting to the changing economic conditions. Matters have been made worse by the fact that a

[2] See similar findings in Chiswick 1986.

disproportionate number of these unskilled Americans are minorities and women. Moreover, as the civil rights movement and the women's movement both have made clear over this same period, both groups are seeking and anticipating changes in their economic and their social status.

How this situation developed and what must be done to correct the nation's immigration policy require careful discussion. Few policy issues are as sensitive and fundamental to the national consciousness as immigration. However, given the challenges presented by the transformation of the US labor market, no relevant aspect of public policy can be immune from a critical examination, no matter how sensitive. The fact is that the mass immigration now facing the nation is a purely policy-driven phenomenon. Immigration itself causes economic change, and it is, therefore, mandatory that the discretionary policies regulating it be consistent with the labor-force needs of the country. As I will show, the prevailing US policies regulating immigration are at total variance with that standard.

2

Mass Immigration and Public Policy

The term "mass immigration" implies that its chief characteristic is quantitative—the size of the annual inflow of foreign-born persons into the population and labor force of the receiving nation. The term also conveys a manifest indifference to the need for congruence between the human capital characteristics of the immigrants and the emerging economic trends or broader social changes at work within the nation.

In 1991, the number of foreign-born persons granted permanent residence status by the United States set an all-time record high for a single year of 1.8 million persons (see table 1). It was the second consecutive year that this record was set and the third straight year that legal immigration exceeded a million people. But these figures underestimate the actual number of foreign-born people entering the country because they take into account neither the number of illegal immigrants who entered nor the number of refugees and asylees who were admitted but who must wait at least a year before they can qualify for resident status. Nor do these figures take into account the growing number of foreign nationals who are legally permitted to work in the United States for specified periods of time (called "non-immigrant workers"). In terms of the total stock of foreign-born persons in the United States, the "official" estimates from the decennial census confirm the post–1965 trend: as shown in table 2, the foreign-born population, which had been declining in both absolute and relative terms since 1920, has steadily increased since 1970. But even these official figures underestimate the true level of the foreign-born population because they also seriously undercount the number of illegal immigrants in the

Table 2. Foreign-Born Population of the United States, 1920–1990

	Number (Millions)	Percentage of Total US Population
1920	14.0	13.2
1930	14.2	11.6
1940	11.6	8.8
1950	10.4	6.9
1960	9.7	5.4
1970	9.6	4.7
1980	13.9	6.2
1990	19.8	7.9

Source: US Bureau of the Census, Washington, DC.

population. An international team of social scientists, commissioned by three large corporations to study broad trends in US society in the 1980s, concludes that "at a time when attention is directed to the general decline in American exceptionalism, American immigration continues to flow at a rate unknown elsewhere in the world" (Oxford Analytica 1986, 20).

The dynamo behind the post–1965 revival of mass immigration to the United States has been federal immigration policy, specifically: the design and implementation of the separate components of the nation's immigration policy; the lack of attention to the collective effects of this policy; and the appalling indifference of policymakers to the unexpected outcomes of their actions. The relevant policy components are those that pertain to legal immigrants, illegal immigrants, refugees, asylees, and temporary foreign workers, who collectively constitute the mass immigration phenomenon of the post–1965 era.

Regardless of the reasons why the mass entry of foreign-born persons for permanent or temporary residence in the United States is either purposely sanctioned or indifferently permitted, all immigrants must be supported, either by their own work or by that of others. Most adult immigrants and their spouses enter the labor market soon after they enter the country, and most of their children eventually do so as well. Hence, there are economic consequences associated with their presence, whether intended or not. As the scale of immigration has increased, it follows that the economic effects, notably on the size and composition of the labor force, also have increased. With immigration currently accounting for 35 percent of the annual growth of the US labor force, it is essential to know how immigrants—regardless of their mode of entry—fit into the labor market. Immigration policy, therefore, must be recognized for what it is: an instrument of economic policy. Unfortunately, policymakers have yet to adopt this perspective when designing the nation's immigration system or assessing the consequences of immigration policy.

In the modern era of sovereign nation-states, immigration has become a discretionary act of governmental policy. Foreign-born persons can enter the territory of another nation to settle permanently or to work temporarily only if they are legally admitted or if the receiving country's government is indifferent to illegal entry or illegal residence. Public policy determines how many foreign-born persons are admitted and under what circumstances. Therefore, immigration policy does not reflect what is happening; it is the institutional arrangement that actually sets the level and shapes the character of the labor market. By the same token, however, immigration is significantly influenced by the historical context from which it evolves.

Although many types of public policy are complex, few are as difficult to comprehend as immigration policy. Indeed, US immigration policy is often compared to the tax code in terms of intricacy, magnitude, and complexity. At the core of US immigration policy are the statutory provisions set forth by Congress, which often are intended to serve multiple purposes and which are influenced both by historical circumstances and by the consensus-building processes within Congress. Once passed, implementation of these statutes is affected by the institutional capacities and practices of the federal agency charged with their administration, the Immigration and Naturalization Service (INS). The INS was housed in the US Department of Labor from the time that department was founded in 1914 until 1940, when it became part of the Department of Justice. Of course, the judiciary resolves disputes over legal meanings and procedural applications and, at times, creates new policy thrusts and administrative obligations.

Just as public policy brought a cessation to mass immigration in the 1920s, it also revived mass immigration in the 1960s and continues to drive the phenomenon in the 1990s. Public policy also will determine how long mass immigration continues and what its effects will be on the nation's economy, population, and labor force into the twenty-first century. As Napoleon once said, "policy is destiny."

Unlike the other major influences affecting the size and composition of the contemporary US labor force—such as the growing labor-force participation of women (especially those with children); the declining labor-force participation of men over age forty-five; the aging of the "baby boom" generation; or the differences in fertility rates among racial and ethnic groups—immigration is purely a policy-driven activity. Immigration is the one element of a nation's labor supply that is a direct consequence of governmental choice; it is neither a necessary nor an inevitable phenomenon. Indeed, no other major industrialized nation has chosen to support mass immigration at this point.

US Immigration Policy before 1965

Mass immigration, of course, has played a significant role in the economic history of the United States. The nation's political ideals, such as freedom, equality under the law, and a toleration of diversity, have long appealed to people from all parts of the globe. Consequently, the United States has never had a problem attracting would-be immigrants when it needed them. But historical and economic circumstances change. While immigration may be both necessary and beneficial at one time, it may not be so at another. Much modern economic analysis is an ahistorical quest to rationalize labor-market trends and to postulate universal principles. But with respect to immigration, an appreciation of historical circumstance is the key to understanding the policies governing the scale and composition of the immigrant flows over time.

In general, prior to World War I, US immigration policy was quite consistent with the development and prevailing labor-force requirements of the US economy. Throughout the first century after independence, the United States had no ceilings on the number and no restrictions on the type of people who were permitted entry for permanent settlement. At this time, the largely preindustrial economy was dominated by agricultural production, and the labor market by agricultural employment. Most jobs required little training or education. Furthermore, the vastness of the land area relative to the population meant that there was little to be done to keep people out, and for the most part, there was little inclination on the part of policymakers even to try. The fact that the amount of "free land" available for settlement expanded throughout most of the nineteenth century also made it difficult to keep significant portions of the native-born population from moving westward. In this era, land was often equated with opportunity.

When industrialization began—slowly before the Civil War but rapidly during and after the war—there was a growing need for nonagricultural workers, and the supply of immigrant workers was intended to fill this demand for labor. A disproportionate number of the immigrants of the nineteenth century were single men for whom family life came only much later, if at all, and so for most immigrants, life as a settler on formerly public lands was not a viable option. With some notable exceptions, therefore, it took a generation or so for most immigrants to accumulate the funds and the knowledge necessary to move inland to settle. Moreover, by 1890, the era of available free land was essentially over, and as the frontier had virtually disappeared, so too had the option of rural settlement for subsequent immigrant streams. Thus, as Stanley Lebergott (1964) writes, "somewhat surprisingly, the greatest beneficiaries of the flow of immigrant labor was never agriculture though farming was our primary industry" in the nineteenth century (p. 28). When the industrialization process began in earnest during the latter decades of the nineteenth century, the new mechanization technology increased the demand for mainly unskilled workers to fill the growing number of manufacturing jobs in the nation's expanding urban areas, as well as to work in mining, construction, and transportation. Immigrants became the major source of workers for the growing urban areas in the North, Midwest, and West. There was still no ceiling on overall immigration, although some qualitative screening had been introduced, e.g., to forbid entry by paupers, prostitutes, and lunatics, regardless of what country they came from, and to forbid entry by Chinese—the first example of ethnic restrictions.

Pools of citizen workers existed who could have been tapped to meet the need for an expanding urban labor force. There were millions of underemployed citizens living and working in the nation's vast rural sector, given the secular decline of the agricultural industry that began in the 1880s. Most notable of these were the millions of freed slaves from the rural South. Indeed, in his famous Atlanta Exposition speech of 1895, Booker T. Washington explicitly pleads with the nation's white industrial leaders to meet their growing urban labor needs by drawing upon the native-born black labor force "whose habits you know . . . whose fidelity and love you have tested . . . [and] who shall stand by you with a devotion that no foreigner can approach." He specifically asks that they not "look to the incoming of those of foreign birth and strange tongue and habits" for their workforce needs. If they do seek to include blacks, he states, we could "make the interests of both races one"; if not, he warns in Cassandra-like terms, it would mean that the future black population would become "a veritable body of death, stagnating, depressing, retarding every effort to advance the body politic" (Washington 1895, 147-48). But his words were not heeded. Instead, mass immigration from Eastern and Southern Europe became the chosen source for the vast majority of new urban workers by the turn of the century (US Immigration Commission 1911, 60, 151, 297–313).

From the standpoint of pure efficiency, the mass immigration of the late nineteenth century and the first fourteen years of the twentieth was consistent with the labor-market needs of the nation. Most of the immigrants were men, whose numbers consistently exceeded the number of women by 2 to 1 and at times by 3 to 1 (for some specific ethnic groups, the male-to-female ratio was as high as 9 to 1). Jobs created during this expansive era typically required little in the way of skill, education, literacy, or fluency in English. The enormous supply of immigrants arriving during this time, who generally lacked these human capital attributes, reasonably matched the prevailing demand for labor. As one scholar of immigration at the time writes: "We may yearn for a more intelligent and better trained worker from the countries of Europe but it is questionable whether or not that type of man would have been so well fitted for the work America had to offer" (Roberts 1913, 363).

With the outbreak of World War I in Europe in 1914, the United States began to experience a sharp contraction in immigration. After the war, when it appeared that mass immigration might resume, the nation imposed its first quantitative restrictions on immigration. An annual ceiling was established of about 154,000 immigrants from the countries of the Eastern Hemisphere, plus their immediate family members (defined as wives and minor children). The pervasive negative social reaction to the pre–World War I immigrants from Eastern and Southern Europe led to the adoption also of overtly discriminatory qualitative screening. Both of these restrictive actions were embodied in the Immigration Act of 1924, often called the National Origins Act.[3] Ethnic screening standards were enacted to favor immigrants from Western and Northern Europe, disfavor all other Europeans, ban virtually all Asians, and ignore most Africans. However, immigration from the Western Hemisphere was not included in either the ceilings or the national-origin quotas in the legislation.

During the 1920s, the domestic economy was expanding rapidly and the assembly line method of production was widely introduced. Adoption of capital-intensive mass-production techniques slowed the hitherto unlimited

---

[3]   For details of the events leading to the passage of the Immigration Act of 1924, see Briggs 1984, 35–38 and 42–46.

demand for workers, although assembly line technology still required workers who were largely unskilled. With mass immigration from the Eastern Hemisphere curtailed, employers turned to surplus domestic labor to meet their needs. The pools of underemployed workers in the massive rural economy finally were tapped, and during the 1920s, the rural population declined in absolute numbers for the first time in the nation's history. Among those who responded to these urban job opportunities were large numbers of native-born blacks from the rural South, who began an exodus to the large cities of the North, the South, and the West Coast. Also during this decade, there was a temporary spurt in immigration from the Western Hemisphere—especially from Canada and Mexico, but also from the Caribbean.

The worldwide Depression of the 1930s, with its massive unemployment, caused immigration from all nations to plummet. Full employment returned with the war during the 1940s, but immigration did not resume. Would-be immigrants from Western and Northern Europe could not leave their countries, and would-be immigrants from the Western Hemisphere were deterred from coming by fears of being drafted into the military. Thus, during the 1930s and 1940s, even the low entry quotas set by the prevailing immigration law were unmet. The labor market of the 1940s was very tight, and the federal government initiated unprecedented policy measures to reduce the artificial barriers to the employment of women, the disabled, youth, older workers, and members of minority groups. Together, these measures opened access for these native-born workers to a wide array of jobs that had been hitherto closed to them.

Pent-up demand for products and forced savings during World War II led to postwar economic prosperity in the late 1940s and the 1950s. It was during these years of general affluence that the civil rights movement launched its assault on all aspects of overt racial discrimination within the United States. This movement culminated in the passage of historic legislation in 1964 regarding public accommodations and employment; in 1965 regarding voting rights; and in 1968 regarding fair housing. Although these laws were primarily directed toward the treatment of black Americans, they also broadened civil rights protection beyond race to include national origin, gender, and religious beliefs. Equal employment opportunity policies subsequently were expanded to protect against discrimination on the basis of age, disability, and alien status. But what is often overlooked is that the path-breaking civil rights legislation of the 1960s was enacted at a time when immigration levels were still sharply restricted. The assumption was that these civil rights laws would terminate discriminatory employment practices and also would be accompanied by policies to promote human resource development for victim groups to redress the past denial of opportunities and to prepare them to qualify for jobs. In the short run, this is, in fact, what occurred. Parallel legislation was adopted in the mid–1960s pertaining to education, training, health, housing, community development, and poverty prevention. With unemployment declining in the mid–1960s, it was assumed that the newly protected groups—blacks in particular—would soon become qualified to fill the jobs that a tightening labor market was making available. The combination of anti-discrimination laws and human-resource-development programs would make the "Great Society" a reality.

In this period of heightened concern over civil rights, it was only natural for the external manifestation of discrimination—the national origins system embodied in the nation's immigration laws—to be a target for reform. It was. But the immigration reform movement of the early 1960s did not include any push to significantly raise the overall level of immigration. It was focused entirely on purging the explicit racism inherent in the national origins admission system. Every President since Harry S. Truman in the late 1940s had sought to do this; it was President Lyndon Johnson who did. The consequences for the level of immigration were entirely unanticipated. Namely, this legislation set in motion forces that triggered a renewal of mass immigration.

The Post–1965 Revival of Mass Immigration

Enactment of the Immigration Act of 1965 ended the era in which immigration policy was a means of racial and ethnic discrimination. But Congress missed an opportunity to craft the new immigration policy so as to meet some positive definition of the public interest. Instead, Congress created a policy that primarily fulfilled the private interests of some legal residents. In the Immigration Act of 1965, the social goals of the national origins admission system were replaced with a politically popular new system based on the concept of family reunification. Seventy-four percent of total visas available each year were reserved for various categories of adult relatives and extended family members of US citizens and permanent resident aliens (in 1980, this percentage was raised to 80 percent). In addition, immediate family members of each adult visa-holder were exempt from all quotas and were usually admitted automatically (this included spouses and minor children, as before, as well as the new category of parents of US citizens). In other words, noneconomic considerations became the guiding principles for the nation's revised immigration policy.

This admission system enjoyed strong support in Congress because it satisfied the personal interests of those citizens who themselves were recent immigrants—the very constituents most likely to have close relatives who were still citizens of other nations. However, there was also a nefarious hidden objective: some interest groups saw family reunification as a way to perpetuate the old national origins systems under a guise that was more politically acceptable. Namely, these groups believed that those racial and ethnic groups that had been discriminated against for the past forty years would be less likely to have living relatives in their homelands than those racial and ethnic groups that had benefited from the national origins system. As the chairman of the House Judiciary Committee and cosponsor of the Immigration Act of 1965, Emanuel Celler (D–NY), stated during the final day of floor debate, "there will not be, comparatively, many Asians or Africans entering the country since the people of Africa and Asia have very few relatives here; comparatively few could immigrate from those countries because they have no family ties to the United States" (*Congressional Record,* 25 August 1965, 21,758). Thus, the adoption of family reunification as the principle criterion for admission meant that satisfying political concerns had replaced pursuit of social ends as the key rationale of the nation's immigration admission system. It remains so today.

The Immigration Act of 1965 also established an annual ceiling of 170,000 visas from all the nations of the Eastern Hemisphere. This figure was slightly higher than the ceiling that had been in effect since the 1920s (156,700 visas plus the immigrants' immediate relatives, which had been expanded in 1952 to include husbands as well as wives and children). The rationale for the slight increase was a recognition that refugee flows in Europe and Asia were a continuing reality and not just a temporary post–World War II phenomenon, and it was hoped that the increase in the Eastern Hemisphere ceiling would absorb such people in the future. With a new annual ceiling on Western Hemisphere visas of 120,000, the total number of visas to be issued in any year was 290,000. The 1965 act also set a ceiling of 20,000 visas for any single country in the Eastern Hemisphere, although no such limit was applied to countries in the Western Hemisphere. A seven-category preference system was created to determine which individuals were to be among the 20,000 admitted from each Eastern Hemisphere nation. Within each category, visas were available on a "first come, first served" basis.

The Johnson administration had strongly supported termination of the national origins system, but it had favored using the needs of the US labor market as the first preference criterion, and it favored issuing the majority of the available visas to fill those labor-market needs. During the legislative process, however, Congress reduced the share of the available visas going to occupational preferences to no more than 20 percent of the total and downgraded the occupational preferences to a lower priority. The most significant shift made by

Congress in the admission priorities, however, occurred with the addition of a new preference category for adult brothers and sisters of US citizens and the assignment of 24 percent of the available visas to such extended family members.

With the imposition of a ceiling on Western Hemisphere immigration, a massive backlog of applications for immigrant visas quickly developed from nations in this region, particularly Mexico. The backlog gave credence to those who had argued that population pressures in Latin America were so strong that without such restrictions there would eventually be a massive migration from these nations to the United States. Given the size of the backlog, the speed with which it developed, and the fact that it was causing hardship for some families that were separated because of it, Congress felt that some sort of mechanism was needed to regulate admissions under the ceiling. Accordingly, in 1976 an amendment was adopted that both extended the seven-category preference system to applicants from the Western Hemisphere and extended the ceiling of 20,000 visas a year to these countries. In 1978, another amendment to the Immigration Act of 1965 finally produced the unified immigration system that reformers had sought for over three decades: the two separate hemispheric ceilings were merged to create a single worldwide annual quota of 290,000 visas. With the amendments in 1976 and 1978, all preferences based on applicants' place of birth had been eliminated; all applicants for legal immigration, regardless of nationality, would be subject to the same admission requirements.

It was not among the objectives of the reform movement of the 1960s to seek any significant increase in the number of immigrants admitted to the United States. There was no general shortage of labor when the new immigration legislation was drafted, debated, and passed. The nation was at war in Vietnam, which had contributed to a decline in the rate of unemployment, but the war was not expected to be long and unemployment was expected to rise once the increased defense expenditures associated with military buildup had passed.[4] Moreover, in 1965, the post–World War II "baby boom" was just beginning to pour into the labor market in unprecedented numbers—a process that would continue unabated for the next fifteen years before tapering off in the 1980s.

Secretary of State Dean Rusk, testifying before Congress in support of the pending reform legislation, stated that "the significance of immigration for the United States now depends less on numbers than on the quality of the immigrants" (US Department of State 1965, 276). Likewise, the floor manager

---

[4] For a background review of labor-force trends and issues in the 1960s and early 1970s, see Killingsworth 1978, 1–13.

for the Senate bill, Senator Edward M. Kennedy (D–MA), echoed this view during the final debate on the pending legislation: "this bill is not concerned with increasing immigration to this country, nor will it lower any of the high standards we apply in selection of immigrants" (*Congressional Record,* 17 September 1965, 24,225). He proved to be wrong on both counts. As shown clearly in table 1, there has been a meteoric growth in legal immigration to the United States since 1965. Mass immigration, with a brazen indifference to the human capital attributes of the immigrants admitted, has been institutionalized.

How is it that mass immigration was revived by reformers who had no such ·objective? The explanation rests with what David North and Marion Houstoun (1976) have aptly described as "negative intent." As they contend, "those interested in reforming the immigration law were so incensed with the ethno-centrism of the laws of the past that they spent virtually all of their energies seeking to eliminate the country-of-origin provisions, and gave very little attention to the substance or long range implications of the policy that would replace them" (p. 5).

As already indicated, the Immigration Act of 1965 did provide for a modest increase in the level of immigration and it did expand the definition of "immediate family," two changes that contributed to the subsequent escalation in immigration. But these are only part of the explanation. Much of the growth in immigration was in the number of immediate family members admitted as immigrants, which reflects the shift in the origin of the majority of the post–1965 immigrants from Europe to Latin America and Asia. The growth in Latin American immigration was caused by widespread use of the family preferences enacted by the new immigration system: Because Latin America had not been covered by the national origins system in effect since 1924, there were many immigrants from this region with living relatives in their homelands who jumped at the opportunity to immigrate to the United States.

The rapid growth in the number of immigrants from Asia is more complicated to explain. The adoption of the family preference system should have worked to prevent an escalation in admission of immigrations from Asia. Indeed, it was anticipated that passage of the Immigration Act of 1965 would lead to a decline in Asian immigration (US Congress 1964, 418). The exclusion of Asians, after all, had been a major reason behind the adoption of the national origin system (as for the earlier Chinese Exclusion Act of 1882; the "Gentle-men's Agreement" with Japan in 1907; and the creation of the "Asiatic Barred Zone" by the Immigration Act of 1917). But Asian immigration did not decline. Through their assiduous use of the occupational preference categories, Asian immigrants entered the United States in increasing numbers after 1965. These immigrants, in turn, were able to use their new citizenship rights to utilize the family reunification priorities and family preference categories to secure entry for members of their immediate and extended families. In addition, Asian immigration soared as a result of an unexpected event that could not have been foreseen in the early 1960s: the Vietnam War. An enormous number of refugees from Southeast Asia were admitted to the United States in the 1970s and 1980s, and once granted permanent resident status and naturalized citizenship, these former refugees used the immigration system to admit their immediate family members and to establish priority immigration entitlements for their adult relatives. As a consequence, Asian immigration accelerated.

Also during the 1960s and early 1970s, the economies of most of the nations of Western Europe were thriving, and so there was little incentive for people from these nations to leave. At the same time, immigration from Eastern Europe was foreclosed by the "Iron Curtain" imposed by the Soviet Union in the late 1940s, which prevented emigration from that region. Hence, by the late 1980s (and continuing into the early 1990s), over 85 percent of immigrants coming to the United States each year were from the countries of Latin America and Asia.

A consequence of the unexpected shift in the origin of immigrants away from Europe to Latin America and Asia after 1965 was a steady rise in the number of immediate family members accompanying each visa-holder (see table 1), and an increase in the size of families with minor children accompanying visa-holders. Moreover, in many of these new source countries, extended families are more prevalent than in Europe, and therefore, the number of parents of US citizens among the immigrant flow also has increased dramatically since 1965, contributing to the overall increase in immigration levels.

Table 1 also shows that the number of immigrants who entered from "other sources" contributed to the post–1965 surge in immigration in a major way. One cause of the growth in this category has been the growth in refugee and asylee admissions. The Immigration Act of 1965 provided for the first time a formal route for certain refugees (17,400 people a year) to be admitted on the basis of humanitarian concerns. To be considered a refugee under the law, however, an applicant must have faced persecution in a nation opposed by the United States (that is, in Communist-dominated nations) or must have been fleeing persecution in countries of the Middle East, not to have faced persecution per se. Hence, even this humanitarian aspect of the law was designed primarily to serve political priorities. However, international events, especially in Cuba and Vietnam, soon led to a rapid escalation in the number of refugees admitted to the United States under the law, to a level that far exceeded the annual ceiling under the Immigration Act of 1965. During this era, an administrative procedure (the "parole authority" exercised by the US Attorney General) and special congressional legislation were used to admit most of the refugees outside of the normal immigration channels.[5] As discussed below, the acceleration of the number of refugees admitted to the United States after 1965 led in 1980 to the removal of refugees from the legal immigration system and the establishment of a separate mechanism for their admission.

The Immigration Act of 1965 also was important for what it did not do. Specifically, it failed to enact any effective measures to enhance its enforcement. Supporters did not foresee the imminent explosion of illegal immigration that quickly ensued passage (see table 3) (Briggs 1992, 150–63). Part of the immediate increase in illegal immigration was due to the fact that the Mexican Labor Program (also known as the "bracero program")—an agricultural labor program authorized during World War II that permitted Mexican nationals to do seasonal agriculture work in the US Southwest—was unilaterally terminated by the United States on 31 December 1964. In 1965, and for several years thereafter, many of these same Mexico nationals (i.e., former "braceros") simply returned to the United States to seek farm work as they had done for more than two decades. This time, however, in doing so they were illegal immigrants, and those apprehended were treated as such.

Several of the provisions of the 1965 act that contributed to the acceleration of illegal immigration had greater long-term effects. The act, it should be recalled, placed a ceiling on immigration from the Western Hemisphere that became effective in mid–1968, which capped the fastest-growing component of the legal immigration stream. In the same vein, when the annual country limit of 20,000 immigrants was extended in 1976 to Western Hemisphere nations, Mexico, in particular, quickly accumulated a massive backlog of would-be emigrants who could not leave legally. Application of the preference system to the Western Hemisphere nations also meant that, for the first time, the only way an individual could qualify for legal immigration was (1) to have a relative who was already a US citizen or a permanent resident alien; (2) to have the specific

---

[5] Only those refugees admitted to the United States under the preference system were automatically eligible to become immigrants after a period of residency. The parole authority, which originally had been intended to apply only to individuals, was extended to massive numbers of refugees, who did not receive immigrant status. Applying individual admission requirements to these parolees would have caused lengthy waiting periods for visas, during which the applicants would have been in limbo. During such an interval, they could not have worked and would have been ineligible for most assistance services. Hence, special legislation was separately enacted for those groups that received parole admissions permitting them to become permanent-residents. For a more complete discussion of the events leading to the emergence of refugees and asylees as a major factor in mass immigration, see Briggs 1992, 121–50.

skills, education, or work experience needed by US employers and, therefore, to qualify for the limited number of work-related visas; or (3) to be a refugee. Once the single worldwide ceiling on immigration went into effect in 1978, no non-preference visas were available for the next ten years. Hence, the only channel available for people who were determined to immigrate but who did not meet any of the three preference requirements was to enter illegally. Hundreds of thousands of people from the Western Hemisphere did just this—especially from Mexico, but also from the British West Indies (after 1962, it became almost impossible for people from these Commonwealth islands to migrate to the United Kingdom), from other Caribbean islands, and from Central and South American countries. Meanwhile, illegal immigration (especially of visa "overstayers") began to increase from nations in the Eastern Hemisphere with which the United States had developed close commercial and/or military relations (e.g., South Korea, Taiwan, Iran, Philippines, and Nigeria). The lack of effective deterrence provided by the Immigration Act of 1965 invited mass abuse—an outcome that for many years policymakers chose to ignore.

Making Matters Worse: The Politics of Immigration Reform

Within a decade after enactment of the Immigration Act of 1965, it was clear that immigration policy had gone seriously awry, and immigration reform was again on the national agenda. In 1978, Congress established the Select Commission on Immigration and Refugee Policy (SCIRP) to study the effects of what had transpired and to make recommendations for change. Appointed by President Jimmy Carter, this sixteen-member commission was chaired by the Reverend Theodore Hesburgh, then president of the Notre Dame University. In its comprehensive report, the Select Commission on Immigration and Refugee Policy (1981) concludes that immigration was "out of control," that the nation must accept "the reality of limitations," and that "a cautious approach" should be taken in the design of any reform measures.

Congress enacted three major immigration statutes: the Refugee Act of 1980 (which relied extensively on the work in progress of SCIRP); the Immigration Reform and Control Act of 1986; and the legislative capstone, the Immigration Act of 1990. Each of these laws embraces some of the specific recommendations put forth by SCIRP, but each goes well beyond SCIRP's recommendations. The overall effect of these laws has been to ignore the "cautious approach" and the modest proposals for immigration increases that were suggested by SCIRP. The result has been a dramatic rise in the already high levels of immigration. Indeed, a 1991 study by the Urban Institute concludes that these statutory changes "have reaffirmed the United States' role as the principal immigrant-receiving nation in the world" (Fix and Passel 1991, 1). The same report finds it "remarkable" that policymakers enacted the Immigration Act of 1990 "with the nation poised on the brink of a recession and a war in the Persian Gulf," and at a time "when other industrialized countries are making [their immigration policies] more restrictive" (p. 9).

The reason Congress could take such "remarkable" expansionary actions is that immigration policy had been allowed to remain decoupled from its economic consequences. Indeed, a better adjective than "remarkable" to describe passage of the 1990 act would be "irresponsible." For in this area of public policy–making, special interest groups with private agendas have captured the process—they simply ignore any consequence for the national interest. The Select Commission on Immigration and Refugee Policy specifically warned of the growing influence of such groups on the policymaking process, and it rejected their myopic appeals. As its report unequivocally states, "the commission has rejected the arguments of many economists, ethnic groups, and religious leaders for a great expansion in the number of immigrants and refugees" (SCIRP 1981, 7). It added that "this is not the time for a large-scale expansion in legal immigration—for resident aliens or temporary workers" (p. 8). The warnings proved to be of no avail. Congress chose to appease the special interest groups. The result is that in the early 1990s immigration policy continues to be essentially a political instrument that is largely unconstrained by the economic environment in which it is applied.

Each of these three major laws requires brief description. The language of the Refugee Act of 1980 did eliminate the ideological biases associated with the definition of refugees under the Immigration Act of 1965. The new definition of refugees embraced the prevailing United Nations definition to include individuals confronted with "a well-founded fear of persecution" on the basis of race, religion, nationality, membership in a particular group, or political opinion. It no longer mattered whether the persecution was threatened or carried out by totalitarian regimes of the political left, the right, or anywhere in between. This law removed refugee admissions from the legal immigration system and, accordingly, reduced the overall annual ceiling on legal immigrants to 270,000 people plus their immediate relatives. The act created a separate admission route for refugees and placed no fixed annual ceiling on their numbers. Instead, the President is empowered to set the annual number of refugees to be admitted, after a largely pro forma consultation with Congress, to reflect his assessment of the world refugee situation. But the number can be influenced by political pressure exerted on the President by domestic special interest groups who empathize with certain foreign groups or their political causes. Consequently, the annual admission figures have ranged from a low of 67,000 in 1986, to a high of 217,000 in 1981. The proposed admission ceiling for 1994 is 121,000 refugees.

The Refugee Act of 1980 also created a new entry mechanism for asylees (aliens who are already in the United States and who qualify for refugee status). The number of asylees admitted each year was exempted from inclusion in the overall immigration ceiling. The number of asylees permitted to "adjust their status" to become permanent resident aliens after a one-year waiting period was originally set at 5,000 asylees a year, and in 1990 was raised to 10,000 per year. Because of the massive backlog of asylee applicants that developed during the 1980s, the ceiling was waived in 1991 to permit adjustment of all eligible asylees whose status was pending as of 1 June 1990. (As a consequence, the number of asylee adjustments in 1991 was 22,664.) No labor-market test is applied to refugee and asylee admissions, although there are obviously labor-market consequences associated with their presence in the US workforce. Since 1980, the preponderance of refugees and asylees have been from Third World nations in Asia, the Caribbean, and Central America. Many others have been from Eastern Europe and the former Soviet Union. Most have been deficient in skills, education, and English-language proficiency. Many have clustered together in a handful of urban enclaves.

The Immigration Reform and Control Act of 1986 (IRCA) was intended to reduce the magnitude of illegal immigration. Among its many provisions, two are of paramount importance. First, to prevent entry of illegal immigrants, civil and criminal sanctions were enacted for the employment of illegal immigrants. Second, as for those illegal immigrants already in the country, four amnesty programs were enacted whose generous provisions were used by over 2.9 million people.

The provisions of the 1986 act relating to employer sanctions were fraught with enforcement loopholes, and by 1990 it was estimated that there were still four million illegal immigrants in the country. Since then, their numbers have continued to mount. Apprehension of illegal aliens by the US Immigration and Naturalization Service, which declined slightly after enactment of IRCA, have soared (see table 3). There are no data on the tens of thousands of illegal immigrants entering the United States each year who are not apprehended. Of course, illegal immigrants enter without regard to whether they are prepared for available jobs or to the possible negative employment effects they might have on citizen workers with comparable skills or education. They seek the most valuable

Table 3. Illegal Aliens Apprehended in the United States, 1961–1991

Year[a]	People Apprehended[b]	
1961	88,823	
1962	92,758	
1963	88,712	
1964	86,597	
1965	110,371	
1966	138,520	
1967	161,608	
1968	212,057	
1969	283,557	
1970	345,353	
Total 1961–70		**1,608,356**
1971	420,126	
1972	505,949	
1973	655,968	
1974	788,145	
1975	766,600	
1976	875,915	
1976-TQ	221,824	
1977	1,042,215	
1978	1,057,977	
1979	1,076,418	
1980	910,361	
Total 1971-80		**8,321,498**
1981	975,780	
1982	970,246	
1983	1,251,357	
1984	1,246,981	
1985	1,348,749	
1986	1,767,400	
1987	1,190,488	
1988	1,008,145	
1989	954,243	
1990	1,169,939	
Total 1981-90		**11,883,328**
1991	1,197,875	

Notes: a. Fiscal years, beginning 1 October as of 1977.
   b. Illegal aliens apprehended by the US Immigration and Naturalization Service.
   c. TQ = transitional quarter when the US government shifted its fiscal year to end on 30 September rather than 30 June.

Source: US Immigration and Naturalization Service, Washington, DC.

economic commodity the US economy has to offer: jobs. The preponderance of illegal immigrants search for work in the low-wage secondary labor market, where, of necessity, they compete with the low-skilled US citizens.[6]

Under the amnesty provisions of the 1986 act, no labor qualifications were imposed on the more than 2.9 million illegal aliens whose entry into the labor force was legalized. As with refugees, most illegal immigrants and amnesty recipients have come from less economically developed nations, and most have similar deficiencies in skills, training, education, and proficiency in English. At the time of their legalization, 78 percent were employed in low-skilled blue-collar occupations, which confirmed the supposition that most illegal immigrants were employed in the secondary labor market (Tienda et al. 1991, 68). They were also found to be clustered, mainly in central urban areas but also in some rural communities where labor-intensive agricultural methods still prevail.

The Immigration Act of 1990 (which went into effect on 1 October 1991) was passed with little public debate and while public attention was diverted by the prolonged and bitter budget battle between President George Bush and Congress. Behind this smoke screen, the legislation was passed on the last day of the 101st session of Congress, and was signed into law by President Bush on 29 November 1990. The most significant feature of this law is its focus on increasing the quantity of immigrants: the level of annual legal immigration was raised to 700,000 people (including immediate relatives), but under certain circumstances the ceiling is "pierceable" if the number of immediate relatives exceeds a specified level in order that they all may be accommodated (see table 4, note c). This represents about a 35 percent increase over the levels prevailing under the Immigration Act of 1965, which the 1990 act replaced. As before, the new law gives short shrift to the specific human capital endowments of most immigrants admitted or to the labor-market conditions of the US economy that prevail at the time of their entry. As shown in table 4, 80 percent of the visas issued each year between 1992 and 1994 (560,000 of 700,000) go to immigrants on grounds that have nothing to do with their employment potential—they are either family immigrants or diversity immigrants. After 1995, the total annual ceiling drops to 675,000 and the percentage of visas reserved for family reunification and diversity declines slightly to 79.2 percent. Thus, the new legislation perpetuates the notion that immigration—despite its magnitude—has little economic impact.

[6]   See North and Houstoun (1976) and Van Arsdol et al. (1979).

The Immigration Act of 1990 did increase the number of immigrants admitted on the basis of occupational needs (i.e., employment-based immigrants) from 54,000 visas a year under the 1965 act to 140,000 visas a year. However, the percentage of visas that are work-related remains the same, 20 percent (140,000 of 700,000). Furthermore, the 140,000 figure grossly overstates the number of work-related immigrants that will be admitted because the number of work-related slots includes not only the eligible workers themselves but also their "accompanying family members." As a result, the number of workers specifically admitted under the work-related provisions will be far fewer—perhaps only one-third of the annual figure of 140,000. Moreover, any work-related slots that are not used in a given year are to be added to those slots available for family-related admissions. Therefore, with the massive backlog of family members and relatives seeking to immigrate that currently exists, it is certain that the ceiling of 700,000 legal immigrants will actually be a floor until such time as the legislation is changed.

In addition, the 1990 law introduces questionable new immigrant categories, such as "investor immigrants," which allows people to "buy their way in," and "diversity immigrants," a category that resurrects one of the most reprehensible features of past US immigration history—the national origin criteria. Visas for diversity immigrants allow admission of people from designated nations from which immigration had been low since 1965 due to the huge backlog of Asians and Latin Americans which had in effect clogged the admission system. There is no labor-market test associated with the admission of diversity immigrants, for whom 40,000 visas a year are available through 1994, after which time the number increases to 55,000 visas a year.

Finally, the immigration system created by the 1990 act permits certain foreign nationals to be legally employed in the United States under specified labor-market circumstances. Known as "non-immigrant workers," their numbers have been growing steadily and are now in excess of 435,000 a year. Although some categories are capped, there are no annual ceilings on the total number of non-immigrant workers who can be admitted. These workers are legally employed in a variety of occupations, including farmworkers, nurses, engineers, professors, and scientists. Most non-immigrant workers can be admitted only if qualified citizen workers cannot be found to fill a job, but typically only perfunctory checks are made to test for citizen availability. The non-immigrant workers supposedly are admitted only for temporary periods, but their visas can be extended in some cases for up to five years. The increasing dependence of US employers on non-immigrant workers is a clear signal that

Table 4. The Preference System Created under the Immigration Act of 1990[a]

	Fiscal Years 1992-1994		Fiscal Years 1995 and beyond	
	Number	Percent	Number	Percent
Family Immigration (Total)	**520,000**	**74.3**	**480,000**	**71.1**
Immediate relatives (projected)	239,000[b]	34.1	254,000[b]	37.6
Preference System (Total)	226,000[c]	32.3	226,000[c]	33.5
Unmarried adult children of US citizens	23,400		23,400	
Immediate family members of permanent residents	114,200[c]		114,200[c]	
Married adult children of US citizens	23,400		23,400	
Brothers and sisters of US citizens	65,000		65,000	
Additional family legalizations[d]	55,000	7.9	0	0
Independent Immigration (Total)	**180,000**	**25.7**	**195,000**	**28.9**
Employment-based immigration	140,000	20.0	140,000	20.74
Priority workers (with extraordinary ability)	40,000		40,000	
Professionals (with advanced	40,000		40,000	
Skilled, professional, and other (unskilled) workers	40,000[e]		40,000[e]	
Special immigrants	10,000		10,000	
Investor immigrants	10,000		10,000	
Diversity immigrants (Total)	40,000[f]	0.57	55,000	8.15
TOTAL ANNUAL IMMIGRATION	**700,000**	**100.0**	**675,000**	**100.0**

NOTES:

a. effective 1 October 1991.

b. The number of immediate family members admitted is unlimited.

c. Because entry of immediate family members is unlimited, the limitation on family immigration is determined by subtracting the total of immediate relatives admitted during the previous year from the worldwide total of family-sponsored immigrants. However, the family preference total is not allowed to fall below 226,000, and therefore the numbers given here are "pierceable" — that is, they may be exceeded if the number of immediate family members admitted is greater than projected.

d. for relatives of IRCA amnesty recipients.

e. limit of 10,000 unskilled.

f. 16,000 must be Irish.

Source: Public Law 101-649.

something is seriously wrong with the current immigration system, namely that the legal immigration system lacks the mandate and the flexibility to respond to legitimate shortages of qualified workers to fill real job vacancies.

In summary, there would be little reason to worry about the employment consequences of such a politically driven policy if immigration were insignificant in size and if the human capital characteristics of those entering were generally consistent with contemporary US labor-market needs. But neither of these conditions is met. The scale of immigration—in all its diverse forms—is without historical precedent. Most immigrants, regardless of mode of entry, are from less economically developed nations, and many lack skills, training, basic education, and proficiency in English. The vast majority have tended to settle in enclaves, primarily in urban areas, and therefore are not easily integrated into the employed workforce. Moreover, the accidental revival of mass immigration occurred just as the US labor market was entering a phase of sustained growth and significant change.

3

The Transformation of the US Labor Force

From 1965 until 1992, the civilian US labor force grew from 74 million workers to 127 million workers—an average of about 2 million workers a year. Mass immigration accounted for an estimated one-third of this labor force growth. Other contributing factors have been the unprecedented entry of women into the labor market and the maturing of the post–World War II "baby boom" generation. Because of their profound economic and social significance, both of these forces require brief discussion.

In both absolute and relative terms, more women have been entering and staying longer in the labor force than at any previous time in the nation's history. The movement has been so abrupt and so large that it can be justifiably described as being a "social revolution." Women comprised 45.3 percent of the civilian labor force in 1990, and it is projected that they will comprise 47 percent by 2000. As shown in table 5, two of every three new entrants to the labor market since 1976 have been women, and this pattern is forecast to continue through 2000. The labor-force participation rate of women has risen from 33.9 percent in 1950 to 57.5 percent in 1990, and as shown in table 5, it is projected to rise to 62.6 percent in 2000. The underlying cause of this growth is the rapidly increasing participation rate of married women in general and of women with children in particular. Single adult women without children have been in the labor market in the past, but the participation of married women and women with children represents a dramatic departure. This shift was completely unpredicted by demographers and labor-market forecasters during the 1960s, at the time when the immigration system was being reformed.

The reasons for the sudden acceleration in the number of women in the labor market are still being debated, but among them are the mechanization of housekeeping tasks since the end of World War II; the growing acceptance of family planning; and the availability of new methods to permit the timing of births. In addition, the civil rights movement provided the momentum to alter the status of women in the workplace in the 1960s. Although women were not initially included in the Civil Rights Act of 1964, opponents of the bill offered an amendment concerning sex discrimination as a ploy to defeat the legislation, and the prohibitions against sex discrimination in employment were included in the final version of the legislation. The moral force of the law, combined with the creation of a legal enforcement mechanism, provided the emerging feminist movement with a lever to attack barriers that previously had prevented women from full participation in the labor market. The pace of change was subsequently enhanced by the prolonged period of high inflation during the 1970s and early 1980s, which decreased real family incomes and forced many women to find jobs in order to maintain their family's standard of living. It is also the case that over this same period there was a surge in the number of households headed by females. In 1989, 16.2 percent of all families were headed by females, up from 10.8 percent in 1970. There are growing numbers of single adult women, and such factors as widowhood, divorce, and pregnancies outside of marriage have left increasing numbers of women as the sole breadwinners for their families. Many such women have been forced to seek employment whether they wished to do so or not (Hayghe 1990, 14–19). Nonetheless, it is highly unlikely that women will abandon the financial and personal independence that they experience when employed, and thus the high labor-force participation of women appears to be a permanent feature of the US economy.

The rapid growth of the US labor force also is partly due to the age distribution of the US population, in particular the large "bulge" in the population—the post–World War II baby boom—between the ages of twenty-five and forty-four, which is now spilling over into the cohort of forty-five- to fifty-four-year-olds. This has been the largest cohort of the population, as well as the fastest-growing, and is comprised of people born between 1946 and 1964. This group has matured into working-age adults, and regardless of gender or race, people between ages twenty-five and forty-four have the highest labor-force participation rates of the entire working-age population.

It is also critical to note that the racial and ethnic composition of the baby boom population is affecting the composition of the labor force. Although family

Table 5. Civilian Labor-force by Sex, Race, and Ethnic Origin, Actual and Projected since 1976[a]

| | Participation Rate (percent) | | | Employment | | | | | | | Annual Employment Growth Rate (percent) | |
| | | | | Level (thousands) | | | Growth (thousands) | | Growth (percent) | | | |
	1976	1988	2000	1976	1988	2000	1976-1988	1988-2000	1976-1988	1988-2000	1976-1988	1988-2000
Working age population[b]	61.6	65.9	69.0	96,158	121,669	141,134	25,511	19,465	26.5	16.0	2.0	1.2
Men	77.5	76.2	75.9	57,174	66,927	74,324	9,753	7,397	17.1	11.1	1.3	0.9
Women	47.3	56.6	62.6	38,983	54,742	66,810	15,759	12,068	40.4	22.0	2.9	1.7
Whites	61.8	66.2	69.5	84,767	104,756	118,981	19,989	14,225	23.6	13.6	1.8	1.1
Men	78.4	76.9	76.6	51,033	58,317	63,288	7,284	4,971	14.3	8.5	1.1	0.7
Women	46.9	56.4	62.9	33,735	46,439	55,693	12,704	9,254	37.7	19.9	2.7	1.5
Blacks	58.9	63.8	66.5	9,565	13,205	16,465	3,640	3,260	38.1	24.7	2.7	1.9
Men	69.7	71.0	71.4	5,105	6,596	8,007	1,491	1,411	29.2	21.4	2.2	1.6
Women	50.0	58.0	62.5	4,460	6,609	8,458	2,149	1,849	48.2	28.0	3.3	2.1
Asians and others	62.8	65.0	65.5	1,826	3,709	5,688	1,883	1,979	103.1	53.4	6.1	3.6
Men	74.9	74.4	74.6	1,036	2,015	3,029	979	1,104	94.5	50.3	5.7	3.5
Women	51.6	56.5	57.5	790	1,694	2,659	904	965	114.4	57.0	6.6	3.8
Hispanics[c]	60.7	67.4	69.9	4,279	8,982	14,321	4,703	5,339	109.9	59.4	6.4	4.0
Men	79.6	81.9	80.3	2,625	5,409	8,284	2,784	2,875	106.1	53.2	6.2	3.6
Women	44.1	53.2	59.4	1,654	3,573	6,037	1,919	2,464	116.0	69.0	6.6	4.5

Notes: a. Moderate growth projected for 1988-2000. b. Age sixteen and over. c. Hispanics may be of any race.
Source: US Department of Labor, Washington, DC.

size is generally decreasing for all major racial and ethnic groups, the decline began earlier and has been more rapid for non-Hispanic whites than for members of minority groups. When combined with the effects of the post–1965 revival of mass immigration, the racial and ethnic composition of the United States population is rapidly changing. Indeed, the 1990 census figures show that the racial composition of the American population changed more dramatically in the 1980s than at any time in the twentieth century (Barringer 1991, A1). During the 1980s, the overall population of the United States increased by 9.8 percent, while the white population grew by 6.0 percent, the black population by 13.2 percent, the Hispanic population by 53.0 percent, the Asian population by 107.8 percent, and the Native American population by 37.9 percent. Population changes influence the size and composition of the labor force. Table 5 shows the anticipated annual growth rates of the number of black, Asian, and Hispanic workers (there is no such data for Native Americans), which considerably exceed those of whites, a trend that is expected to continue into the twenty-first century (Kutscher 1991, 6–7).

The combined influences of these forces—mass immigration, demographics, and the women's movement—has meant that there has been no general shortage of labor since 1965 that might warrant the dramatic increase in immigration that has been permitted to occur. It is true that the US Department of Labor has projected a slight decline in labor-force growth (to about 1.6 million workers a year) during the 1990s (see table 5), but this still means that the labor force will add 19.5 million workers to its ranks during the decade (Fullerton 1989; see also Pear 1992). This "official" growth projection for the 1990s, however, grossly understates immigration flows at the time and was made obsolete by subsequent legislative developments. To be specific, the Department of Labor projections, made in 1988, estimate that 100,000 illegal immigrants would enter the country each year during the 1990s—a figure now known to be several multiples of this figure—and they make no allowance for the more than 2.9 million former illegal immigrants who received amnesty since 1988 or for the enormous family reunification implications of each individual amnesty adjustment. The projections estimate annual legal immigration at 400,000, when the figure was over 500,000 at the time; annual immigration has now risen to 700,000 under the Immigration Act of 1990. Finally, the projections make no allowance for annual refugee admissions. In all likelihood, labor-force growth for the 1990s will approach the record levels of the 1980s and will certainly exceed the official projections. When this sustained growth in the labor force is combined with the underutilization of labor implicit in the persistent unemployment rates of about 7.5 percent that prevailed in the early 1990s, it is inconceivable that the United States will have a general shortage of potential workers over the remainder of the 1990s.

In addition to the sustained growth of the labor force, the US labor market also is in a period of radical transformation. The demand for labor is being affected by restructuring forces stemming from the nature and pace of technological change; from the stiff international competition the United States now confronts for the first time in its history; from major shifts in consumer spending away from goods toward services; and from the substantial reduction in national defense expenditures brought about by the end of the Cold War in the early 1990s.[7] Without elaborating on the specific effects of each of these powerful and unprecedented forces, suffice to say that they are reshaping the nation's occupational, industrial, and geographic employment patterns.

As discussed earlier, the mass immigration experienced in the United States during the late nineteenth and early twentieth centuries occurred at a time when producing goods was the dominant employment sector of the US economy. Since the end of World War II, the goods-producing sector has ceased to grow. In fact, as shown in table 6, the percentage of total employment in the goods-producing sector has been falling steadily. As indicated, in 1990, 77.3 percent of the nonagricultural labor force was employed in the service industries. Moreover, the US Department of Labor has projected that 90 percent of the jobs to be created in the 1990s will be in the service industries (Personick 1987). The emergence of the service economy has imposed an entirely different set of job requirements on the actual and potential labor force: while the technology of earlier periods (when the goods producing industries were expanding) stressed physical and manual skills for job-seekers, the emerging service-producing economy has since the 1960s created jobs that stress mental, social, linguistic, and communication skills. A premium is placed on cognitive skills such as reading, writing, numeracy, and fluency in English.

Of even greater significance than the industrial shifts in employment are the radical changes that are taking place concurrently in the occupational patterns of employment. Table 7 shows the increasing percentage of employment in the non-production occupations (i.e., white-collar jobs) and the declining percentage of employment in the production occupations (i.e., blue-collar jobs) in every industrial sector. It is in table 8, however, that the consequences of the

---

[7] For a detailed discussion of the causative factors and characteristics of this transformation, see Briggs 1992, chap. 7.

Table 6. Non-farm Employment in Goods-Producing and Service-Producing Sectors, 1950–1990

| | Total | Level (thousands) | | Percent | |
		Goods-Producing	Service-Producing	Goods-Producing	Service-Producing
1950	45,222	18,775	26,447	41.6	58.4
1960	54,234	20,393	33,841	37.6	62.4
1970	70,920	23,508	47,412	33.1	66.9
1980	90,405	25,658	64,747	28.4	71.6
1990	110,330	25,004	85,326	22.7	77.3

Source: US Council of Economic Advisers, *Economic Report of the President, 1991.* (Washington, DC: US Government Printing Office, 1991).

Table 7. Private-Sector Employment in Non-production or Supervisory Occupations, 1950-1990
(percent of total)

	1950	1960	1970	1980	1990
Goods-Producing Industries					
Mining	9.4	19.9	24.1	25.8	28.0
Construction	11.1	14.7	16.7	21.3	23.0
Manufacturing	17.8	25.1	27.5	29.9	32.1
Service-Producing Industries					
Transportation, Communication, and Public Utilities	n.a.	n.a.	13.3	16.6	16.9
Wholesale Trade	9.6	13.9	16.6	18.2	19.8
Retail Trade	5.6	7.5	9.1	10.2	11.5
Finance, Insurance, and Real Estate	17.1	18.4	21.0	24.3	27.4
Personal Services	n.a.	n.a.	9.2	11.0	12.8

n.a. = not available

Source: US Department of Labor, Washington, DC.

occupational restructuring of the US economy are most vivid. From 1978 to 1990, when the number of employed persons in the labor force increased by an incredible 22.1 percent, the distribution of occupational growth was sharply skewed. The share of overall employment growth was the greatest for the occupations that required the highest levels of training and the most extensive amounts of education (e.g., executive, manager, administrator, professional, and technical occupations), which accounted for over half of all job growth over this period. Conversely, the share of employment growth was the smallest for those occupations that entail the least job preparation. Indeed, all of the unskilled occupations—private household workers, laborers, and farmworkers—experienced negative growth over this period. In other words, low-skilled jobs are rapidly disappearing from the US economy.

The emerging employment structure of the United States is debunking the pervasive myth that service-sector jobs are dead-end and low-paying. Of course, some are, just as some jobs in the goods-producing sector are, such as agricultural work and textile and garment manufacturing. But the reality is that 80 percent of the professional and managerial jobs in the economy are to be found in the service sector. And while it is true that there are growing employment opportunities in such low-paying service industries as fast-foods and nursing home care, there are also substantial increases in employment in high-paying jobs in computer services, legal services, and advertising, as well as in average-paying jobs in insurance, wholesale trade, and auto repair.

In its projections of occupational growth to 2000, the US Department of Labor forecasts that the managerial, professional, and technical occupations—all of which require postsecondary levels of education and training—are expected to continue to grow much faster than total employment (Silvestri and Lukasiewicz 1987). Of the twenty occupations projected to grow fastest in the 1990s, half are related to the growing computer and health fields. The shift to a service-based economy is leading to a general upgrading of the skills and education required of the labor force. Conversely, of course, those occupations that require minimal skills and education have sharply contracted and are projected to continue to do so.

Employment patterns in the United States also are undergoing significant geographic shifts. The expansion of nonagricultural employment in the United States is extremely unbalanced (Rones 1986). The greatest employment growth in the 1970s and 1980s occurred in the South Atlantic region (from Delaware to Florida), West South Central region (from Arkansas to Texas), and the Pacific Coast. The greatest declines in employment have been in the mid-Atlantic region (New York, New Jersey, and Pennsylvania) and East North Central region (the

Table 8. Growth and Share of Major Occupational Groups, 1978–1990

	Increase or Decrease (percent)	Percent Share of Employment Increase or Decrease
Executive, Manager, and Administrator	56.7	25
Professional	42.3	22
Technical	45.8	5
Sales	36.7	18
Administrative Support	18.4	13
Protective Services	35.9	2
Private Household	-26.1	-1
Other Services	24.3	12
Precision Production and Craft	13.9	8
Machine Operator	-10.0	-4
Transportation Operatives	7.9	2
Laborers	-3.9	-1
Farm, Forestry, and Fishing	-7.9	-1
Total US Occupational Growth	**22.1**	**100**

Source: John H. Bishop and Shani Carter, "How Accurate Are Recent BLS Occupational Projections?" *Monthly Labor Review* (October 1991), 38.

Great Lakes area from Wisconsin through Ohio). These employment shifts reflect the broader movement of the population away from the Northeast and Midwest to the Southeast and West.

The 1990 census also revealed that, for the first time in the nation's history, more than half the population lived in the thirty-nine large metropolitan areas that have populations of one million or more (Vobejda 1991a). In 1950, 30 percent of the population lived in such areas; in 1980, 46 percent did; and in 1990, slightly over 50 percent did. Of these thirty-nine large metropolitan areas, 90 percent grew in size during the 1980s. The greatest growth came in the metropolitan areas in the South Atlantic states (nine of the twelve fastest-growing metropolitan areas in the nation were in Florida) and in the Pacific Coast states. The growth in metropolitan areas, however, occurred primarily in the suburbs, not in the central cities. Of the five largest metropolitan areas that lost populations, four (Pittsburgh, Buffalo, Cleveland, and Detroit) were in the former manufacturing heartland bordering the Great Lakes. The only other metropolitan area whose population declined over the decade was New Orleans. Implicit in the proportional growth of all metropolitan areas, of course, is the proportional decline in nonmetropolitan (i.e., rural) areas.

It has already been noted that the labor force in the United States has been growing at a rate that is far faster than the combined rate of all its major industrial competitors and that it is without precedent in US history. It has also been demonstrated how the composition of the US labor force is changing, with the fastest-growing segments of the labor force comprised of women, minorities, and immigrants. These are the very segments of the workforce—women in general and minorities in particular (with the possible exception of Asian Americans)—that have had fewer opportunities to be trained, educated, or prepared for the occupations that are predicted to increase most in the coming decade and which are disproportionately concentrated in occupations and industries already in decline or which are most vulnerable to decline in the near future (Cyert and Mowry, chap. 5).

4

The Conflict between Immigration Policy and Emerging Economic Trends

When Congress embarked in the 1960s on the course of adopting a politically driven immigration policy, few people recognized that the country was entering a period of such fundamental economic change and labor-market restructuring. Even after the new employment trends became evident in the 1980s, the congressional committees responsible for designing immigration policy ignored them, as vividly demonstrated by the incongruity of the provisions of the Immigration Act of 1990 with these trends.

By definition, immigration policy can influence the quantitative size of the labor force as well as its qualitative characteristics. Currently, there is little synchronization of immigrant flows with the demonstrated needs of the labor market. With widespread uncertainty as to the number of immigrants who will enter the United States in any given year, it is impossible to know in advance how many foreign-born people will enter the US labor force annually. Moreover, whatever skills, education, linguistic abilities, talents, or geographic settlement preferences immigrants and refugees possess are largely incidental to the rationale and means of their entry, whether legal or illegal.

Table 9 shows the occupations of the immigrants at the time of arrival for selected years since 1970. While admittedly crude, this administrative data are sufficient to show broad trends and rough orders of magnitude, and they show that the labor-market effects of the politically driven immigration system are twofold.

Table 9. Distribution of Immigrants by Major Occupation at Time of Arrival, Selected Fiscal Years 1970–1991

	1970	1975	1979[a]	1985	1989	1990	1991
Total Immigrants	373,326	386,194	530,639	570,009	1,068,342	1,536,483	1,827,167
Professional, Technical, and Kindred Workers	12.3	9.9	8.6	7.3	4.2	4.4	3.2
Managers, Officials, and Proprietors (excluding Farmworkers)	1.6	2.6	4.0	3.6	3.0	3.0	1.5
Clerical and Kindred Workers	3.7	3.8	4.6	3.4	4.2	3.7	1.7
Sales Workers	0.7	0.9	1.0	2.1	2.0	2.0	1.1
Craftsmen, Foremen, and Kindred Workers	7.5	5.5	4.4	4.6	6.4	7.3	2.9
Operatives and Kindred Workers	4.9	4.8	6.6	8.5	15.7	15.9	5.5
Laborers (excluding Farmworkers and Mineworkers)	3.8	3.4	3.0				
Private Household	2.7	1.5	1.9	7.5	12.8	14.9	5.2
Service Workers (excluding Private Household)	2.5	4.2	3.5				
Farmers and Farm Managers	1.0	0.2	0.2	1.9	2.9	6.8	51.0
Farm Laborers and Foremen	1.2	1.6	2.1				
No Occupation[b]	57.9	61.3	59.8	61.1	48.5	41.7	27.8

Notes: a. Occupational data for 1980 and 1981 were lost in INS data processing. See *Statistical Yearbook of the INS, 1981* (Washington, DC: U.S. Government Printing Office, 1982), vii.

b. Includes dependent women and children and other aliens without occupation or occupation not reported.

Source: U.S. Immigration and Naturalization Service, Washington, DC.

On the one hand, some immigrant and non-immigrant workers have human capital endowments that are quite congruent with the emerging labor-market needs. Some have the education, skills, and work experience that are desperately needed to fill vacant jobs in the expanding sectors of the economy, which in part result from an appalling lack of attention by policymakers to the inadequate preparation of citizens for the jobs created by the changing labor market. However, even when legitimate labor shortages exist, immigration should never be allowed to dampen two types of market pressures: those needed to encourage citizen workers to invest in preparing for vocations that are expanding; and those needed to ensure that governmental bodies provide the human-resource-development programs needed to prepare citizens for the new types of jobs that are emerging. First recourse always should be to retrain and reeducate unqualified workers and to relocate unemployed and underemployed qualified workers. As the Commission on Workforce Quality and Labor Market Efficiency (1989) strongly warns in its report to the US secretary of labor, "by using immigration to relieve shortages, we may miss the opportunity to draw additional US workers into the economic mainstream" (p. 32). It goes on to state that public policy should "always try to train citizens to fill labor shortages" (p. 32). This fundamental principle of priority-setting is presently missing in the nation's immigration policies.

On the other hand, the data in table 9 clearly show that the occupations of the legal immigrants, refugees, asylees, and others who have been allowed entry to the United States are essentially mirror opposites of those occupations shown earlier in table 8 to be experiencing the greatest growth. The data reflect the results of an admission system that is not based on the work-related needs of the economy. Since the post–1965 wave of mass immigration began, the proportion of immigrants whose occupations at the time of arrival were in the professional, technical, or managerial occupations has declined sharply, although it is precisely these occupations that have sustained the greatest growth over this period. Likewise, the occupations of the preponderance of new immigrants have been either in blue-collar goods-producing jobs (operatives, laborers, and farmworkers) or low-wage personal service jobs—precisely the occupations that have experienced the sharpest decline over this period. Indeed, it is mind-boggling to see in table 9 that over half of the 1.8 million immigrants (932,606 to be exact) who were granted permanent resident status in 1991 reported their occupation as farmworker! No occupation in the US economy has workers with lower levels of educational attainment or lower skill requirements than farm work, and agriculture as an industry has been a declining source of jobs for over forty years.

In urban areas, the entry of so many low-skilled immigrants and their family members—especially those who have entered illegally—are a major cause of the revival of "sweatshop" enterprises and the upsurge in the child labor violations.[8] It is not surprising, therefore, that research by George Borjas (1990) and Barry Chiswick (1986) on the economic impact of immigrants finds that the human capital characteristics of the post–1965 immigrant population has been rapidly declining. Thus, precisely when the nation needs a more highly skilled and better educated labor force, US immigration policy is supplying large numbers of unskilled, poorly educated workers who have a limited ability to speak English to the central cities of many major urban labor markets, where they compete with the sizable pool of low-skilled citizen workers for a declining numbers of jobs in low-skill sector of the labor market. In such an environment, it should not be surprising to learn that for those workers who lack skills and are poorly educated who do find jobs, real wages were depressed during the 1980s (Bound and Johnson 1992).

It needs also to be noted that the data in table 9 probably overstate the positive occupational characteristics of the flow of post–1965 immigrants because the data do not include the characteristics of the ongoing massive infusion of illegal immigrants; those who enter as refugees (mostly from Third World nations) but who have not yet adjusted their status to become permanent resident aliens; or those who legally work as non-immigrants. As discussed earlier, studies that have focused on determining the characteristics of illegal immigrants find them to have minimal human capital endowments and to be overwhelmingly employed in blue-collar and service occupations in low-wage sectors of the economy (North and Houstoun 1976, 104; Van Arsdol et al. 1979, 69). These findings have been confirmed in the data collected on illegal immigrants who benefited from legalization under the Immigration Reform and Control Act of 1986 (see US Immigration and Naturalization Service 1992, 70; Tienda et al. 1991). Likewise, the available data on the human capital charac- teristics of refugees also reveal minimal human resource endowments as well as

---

[8]   For example, see "ILGWU Expands Campaign Against Sweatshops," *AFL–CIO News* (14 May 1990), 7; Constance Hays, "Immigrants Strain Chinatown's Resources," *New York Times* (30 May 1990), B1, B4; Peter T. Kilborn, "Tougher Enforcing of Child Labor Laws Is Vowed," *New York Times* (8 February 1990), A22; Peter T. Kilborn, "Widespread Child Labor Violations," *New York Times* (16 March 1990), A10; Lisa Belkin, "Abuses Rise Among Hispanic Garment Workers," *New York Times* (28 November 1990), A16; and Donatella Lorch, "Immigrants from China Pay Dearly to be Slaves," *New York Times* (3 January 1991), B1.

high unemployment, low labor-force participation, and a high incidence of welfare dependency.[9] The occupational data for non-immigrants, as could be expected, is quite mixed, as they have been employed in a variety of occupations including farmworker, nurse, engineer, scientist, executive, manager, and professor. Indeed, as mentioned above, a major reason for the growth in the use of non-immigrant workers by US employers is that there have been so few work-based visas available under the current immigration system.

Given the substantial size of the immigrant population and the overwhelming tendency of immigrants to concentrate in the urban areas and especially the central cities of about six states (California, New York, Texas, Florida, Illinois, and New Jersey), there should be concern over their impact on citizens and resident aliens who also seek employment in these labor markets. It is not only the actual effects of increased competition for jobs and social services that are important. There is the opportunity cost. What would have happened to the employment opportunities of citizens had immigrants not congregated in significant numbers in these labor markets? Would there have been an impetus for public and private policies to provide quality education and training to citizen workers (as they were during World War II) if the alternative supply of immigrant labor were less available? Would the adjustment process associated with the transformation of the economy have led to a greater inflow of displaced citizens into these same local labor markets if immigrant labor was not there? Would fewer citizens and resident aliens have left these labor markets without the immigrant inflows?

There have been a number of studies that have tried to determine ex post the multiple effects of post–1965 immigration on specific labor markets and on the US economy as a whole.[10] All of these studies are plagued by the gross inadequacies of available data. A special committee that was chosen by the National Research Council of the National Academy of Sciences to study the quality of immigration data reports that:

[9] See US Coordinator for Refugee Affairs (1992, 32). In this report, a survey of the labor-force status of refugees found their unemployment rate was 14 percent—over twice the US average—and their labor-force participation rate was only 36 percent, compared to 66 percent for the nation as a whole. The anticipated costs for resettlement of refugees in 1993 was over $500 million.
[10] For example, see Bailey 1987; Bogen 1987; Borjas 1990; Bouvier 1986, 1991a; Bouvier and Briggs 1988, chap. 6; Bouvier and Weller 1992; and Muller and Espenshade 1985.

Immigration, for some reason, is the Cinderella of the federal statistical system. In essence, a history of neglect has afflicted the record keeping concerning one of the most fundamental processes underlining the development of American society. (National Research Council 1985, 3)

Most of the impact studies are forced to use census data on the foreign-born population, which unfortunately do not distinguish between the route used by such people to enter the United States. All immigrants are lumped together so as to create a statistical composite that does not reflect the range of differences between immigrants, illegal immigrants, refugees, asylees, or non-immigrants. Also, of course, the data only include those who are counted by the census, and it is well known that many illegal immigrants are missed.

Multiple influences other than immigration affect employment, wage, and income experiences—such as short-run cyclical swings or long-run structural shifts in the economy—and these make it difficult to isolate the specific effects of immigrants in local or national labor markets. For instance, two important studies on the effects of immigration on the economy of California, one by the RAND Corporation (McCarthy and Valdez 1985) and another by the Urban Institute (Muller and Espenshade 1985), claim to find only minor adverse effects. These studies, however, have been severely criticized by Ray Marshall (1988), who convincingly shows that "their conclusions often do not follow from their evidence" (p. 195). From his analysis of both studies, Marshall finds that "there can be little doubt that immigration displaces workers," that "no study of the effects of immigration is able to hold everything constant," and that "elementary economics suggests that at a time of high unemployment, increased labor supplies depress wages and reduce employment opportunities for legal residents unless you completely segregate labor markets" (p. 195). Likewise, the usefulness of impact studies is hampered by the fact that they cannot measure what would have happened if the immigrants were not present. For example, there is no way for a local labor market study to measure the effects on citizen workers who have left high immigrant-impacted communities for just that reason. Moreover, there would have been alternative adjustment patterns, as there were when industries and occupations declined in other geographic regions, in many of the nation's largest urban labor markets were it not for the fact that they became mass immigrant centers in the interim. Likewise, there is mounting anecdotal evidence in the highly immigrant-impacted states that immigration is causing severe adjustment difficulties and fiscal distress even if these effects have yet to be discerned in academic impact studies, which by definition must lag years behind actual events.[11] In fact, all of the key academic studies to date have used 1980 census data, which precede the decade in which the United States experienced the highest level of immigration in its history.

What the nation faces is a shortage of *qualified* labor. The appropriate policy would be to address the mounting mismatch between the skills of citizens and the emerging skills and education requirements of the workplace. In other words, an expanded national human-resource-development policy for citizen workers is required. In this context, there is certainly no need for an immigration policy that annually encourages or tolerates the mass entry of immigrants with only minimal regard to their human capital attributes or which places additional remedial burdens on an already underfunded and inadequate education and training system.

---

[11]   For example, see Miles 1992; Robert Reinhold, "In California, New Talk about a Taboo Subject," *New York Times* (3 December 1991), A20; "Business Abandons Paradise,"*Rocky Mountain News* (18 July 1991), 65; Joseph N. Boyce, "Struggle over Hospital in Los Angeles Pits Minority Versus Minority," *Wall Street Journal* (1 April 1991), A1, A4; and David Gonzales, "Criticisms Aimed at Statements on Immigrants," *New York Times* (5 October 1990), B3.

5

The New Social Environment

The rekindling of the forces of mass immigration in the mid–1960s coincided with achievement of the legislative goals of the civil rights movement. The immigration reform movement and the civil rights movement shared a common concern for the elimination of discriminatory influences in American society, but it was clearly unforeseen that these two powerful movements for social change could collide, as they have.

The civil rights movement of the 1960s was focused primarily on the status of black Americans. No other group has had to endure the pangs of both slavery and de jure segregation. Since the founding of the nation—when the Constitution permitted blacks to be counted as only three-fifths of a person in apportioning representatives to the House of Representatives and specifically allowed slave trading to continue for twenty more years as the political price of unifying the thirteen original colonies—no issue of domestic welfare has proved more challenging to overcome nor more obligatory to address. There are clear signs that the economic status of black Americans has deteriorated since the revival of mass immigration in the mid–1960s. While a complete discussion of this issue is beyond the scope of this essay, the issue cannot be ignored. Indeed, there is every reason to fear that mass immigration has adversely affected the economic status of blacks, especially those working in urban areas.

Buried within the statistical data on labor-force trends contained in table 5 is one deeply worrisome development: the low labor-force participation rate of black males relative to white males. Historically, through the 1940s, the labor-force participation rate of black males consistently exceeded that of white males, but in the 1950s, the rate for white males surpassed the black rate and the gap between the two has widened since. In 1990, the rate for white males exceeded the rate for black males by 6.8 percent (76.9 percent to 70.1 percent). The wide gap exists for every age subgroup. Indicative of the significance of this decline in black male labor-force participation is the fact that in 1990 the absolute number of black women in the labor force exceeded that of black men (6,785,000 black women to 6,708,000 black men). Blacks are the only racial group in the US labor force for which this is true, and, as is also shown in table 5, the difference is projected to worsen throughout the 1990s. Black women now constitute the largest minority group in the US labor force. On the surface, there is no reason why white males should have a significantly higher participation rate for every age cohort than black males or why white males should have a considerably higher overall rate. In fact, given that the black population is considerably younger than the white population (the median age of the white population in 1988 was 33.2 years while it was 27.5 years for blacks), standard labor-market analysis would predict that the black male labor-force participation rate would be higher than the comparable white rate. However, blacks are clustered disproportionately in locations where jobs are frequently scarcest—in the central cities of twelve major urban areas outside the South, in cities in the South, as well as throughout the rural South (the only region with a significant rural black presence). Moreover, black male workers have been disproportionately displaced by the decline in manufacturing industries and production-related occupations because they were disproportionately employed in these sectors (Kletzer 1991). These are precisely the same industries and occupations in which post–1965 immigrants have been clustered (see table 9).

The low participation rate reflects, in part, the fact that black male unemployment is about twice that of white males, but low participation rates also mean that a significant number of black males simply have stopped looking for work or that they do not actively seek work. The question then is, if these adult black males are not at work, in school, or in the military, what are they doing to survive? The answer, of course, is that an urban subclass of adult black males who function outside the normal labor market has been formed and institutionalized (Wilson 1987; see also Uchitelle 1987). Many of these men exist through reliance on irregular activities such as casual "off the books" work and anti-social behavior such as crime. They may engage in such self-destructive activities as alcoholism, drug abuse, and violence.

There is an even more troublesome factor involved, namely that an inordinately high number of black males are incarcerated in federal and state prisons as well as in local jails (in 1988 almost one-half of those incarcerated were black). These people are not even included in the labor-force participation data, which includes only the non-institutionalized proportion of the black male population over the age of sixteen.

Of course, the worsening economic plight of black males also affects black females in particular and the black family structure in general. Up until the 1950s, black women married at higher rates than white women, but by 1991, the proportion of black women who had never married had reached an incredible figure of 25 percent—three times higher than the comparable percentage for white women (Vobejda 1991b). The major explanation rests with the fact that the pool of black men who are able to earn a living through work in the regular economy sufficient to support a family is rapidly shrinking. It is not only the negative effects of being disproportionately employed in low-wage occupations, or the high incidence of unemployment, or the inordinately high incarceration rates of black men, it is also the soaring death rate—especially from homicide—of urban black males (Vobejda 1991b). The effects on the black family structure have been devastating. In 1990, 57.6 percent of all black births were out of wedlock, compared to 17.2 percent for whites and 23.2 percent for Hispanics (Pear 1992; see also Taylor 1991). Female heads of households with families, especially those from minorities groups, are usually condemned to lives of poverty, as are their offspring.

A major reason why black male labor-force issues have not been satisfactorily addressed has been the availability of the large flows of immigrant workers since 1965 into many of the same labor markets where the urban black population is concentrated. As Elizabeth Bogen (1987) succinctly observes, post–1965 mass immigration, like earlier waves of mass immigration, "is overwhelmingly an urban phenomenon" (p. 60). The 1980 census disclosed that 92 percent of the foreign-born population lived in metropolitan areas, compared to 74 percent of the native-born. More to the point, 40 percent of the foreign-born population lived in only five metropolitan areas—New York, Los Angeles, Chicago, San Francisco, and Miami—whereas only 11 percent of the native-born population lived in these areas. Eight central cities—the five listed above plus Houston, San Diego, and Philadelphia—accounted for 26 percent of the entire foreign-born population. All eight of these central cities also have substantial black populations. Given the high levels of immigration that occurred during the 1980s, it is certain that the 1990 census data, available in late 1993, will show even higher concentrations of foreign-born in these eight central cities and probably in several others as well. The mass entry of immigrants into these central cities has increased the competition for available jobs. Under these conditions, an inordinate number of black males apparently have despaired of seeking work in the regular economy.

Competition from immigrants, while not the only factor to explain the low labor-force participation rates of black males, must be included within any such list of negative influences. The adverse impact of mass immigration on the employment of blacks has been highlighted by studies of the 1992 urban riots in Los Angeles (Miles 1992). As one observer of those events cogently writes:

> Over the last decade, powerful demographic forces began to change the urban complexion. Enormous waves of foreign immigrants arrived and began to push blacks out of Watts. Between the 1980 and 1990 censuses, the black population of Los Angeles County dropped from 13 percent to 11 percent of the population, while both the Hispanic population and the Asian population swelled. (Reinhold 1992)

Proving direct job displacement is difficult because it requires either detailed case studies or local labor-market data that is focused on central cities rather than on broad metropolitan areas, and such data either presently does not exist or is unreliable. There is, however, one rare specific case study of southern California that clearly documents a situation in which black janitorial workers, who had successfully built a strong union in the 1970s that provided high wages and good working conditions, was almost totally displaced in the 1980s by Hispanic immigrants, who were willing to work for far lower pay and fewer benefits (Mines and Avina 1992). After an analysis of the expanding labor force over the 1980s in Los Angeles and Santa Clara counties, Mines and Avina find conclusively that "the deterioration of wages, working conditions, and union strength in California's janitorial industry over the decade reflects changing market conditions and non-union contractors timely adaptation to the large scale availability of recently arrived immigrants" (p. 430).

Studies of the New York City labor market, which is the nation's largest single labor market and also has highest absolute number of foreign-born persons of any US city, find that immigrant workers are clustered in only a few industries. One study (Bogen 1987) finds that almost half (47 percent) of all post–1965 immigrants in the city were employed in only thirteen industries, out of over 200 industries for which census data is collected. The study adds that, because of the acknowledged undercounting of illegal immigrants, "the concentration of immigrants in those industries may be even higher than census data suggests" (pp. 84–85). These thirteen industries, moreover, accounted for an incredible 35 percent of all employed persons in the city. Another study (Bouvier and Briggs 1988) finds the preponderance of the post–1965 foreign-born workers in the city were concentrated in generally low-paying industries such as apparel manufacturing, hospitals, eating and drinking establishments, private household work, hotels, and nursing facilities. In viewing these findings in the context of the overall New York City labor market, the authors candidly conclude that,

> With immigrant concentrations of this magnitude, it is hard to argue that the presence of immigrant workers is not affecting both wage trends and employment opportunities in these particular industries over what might prevail in their absence. (Bouvier and Briggs 1988, 61)

Furthermore, these studies were based on data from the 1980 census, which (as noted above) do not reflect the largest infusion of new immigrants in the nation's history which occurred in the 1980s. Hence, as the authors of the study cited above of the city's overall labor market warn, "it is likely that the 1990 census will reveal even larger concentrations of immigrant workers in these industries" (Bouvier and Briggs 1988, 61).

There is also evidence that new immigrants who have opened their own businesses in cities and who themselves become employers are actively discriminating against native-born workers—especially blacks—in hiring. In her study of New York City, Bogen (1987) candidly writes, "there are tens of thousands of jobs in New York City for which the native born are not candidates" (p. 91). The reasons she cites are that "ethnic hiring networks and the proliferation of immigrant-owned small businesses in the city have cut off open-market competition for jobs" and that the blatant "discrimination against native workers is a matter for future monitoring" (p. 91). The issue of employment discrimination also surfaced as a significant cause of the racial tension in Los Angeles between native-born blacks and new immigrants that erupted in the spring of 1992 in the worst urban riot in the nation's history (Miles 1992). Research in those rural labor markets where immigrant workers have become a significant factor (e.g., in the agriculture industry of the Southwest) also reveals the widespread use of ethnic networking in the hiring process (Mines and Martin 1983, 139, 149). The negative effects on the employment of native-born workers in these rural areas is the same as in urban labor markets. The concept of networking is highly praised by many scholars who study the current immigrant experience, but what is overlooked in these studies is that these practices—the use of national origin as a factor to favor or to deny employment opportunities—is specifically banned by the Civil Rights Act of 1964. What was legally permissible at the beginning of the twentieth century is illegal now at its end.

It is certain that blacks in many urban areas have been adversely affected by discrimination by immigrant employers, and it is highly likely that they have been adversely affected by the competition for jobs with post–1965 immigrants. This seems even more likely given the concentration of both immigrants and blacks in the same industrial sectors. Proving direct displacement, however, is not easy because it is not possible to measure what would have happened absent mass immigration. Would blacks have continued to migrate into the cities to fill jobs if immigrants had not moved in? Would blacks have stopped moving out of urban areas if mass numbers of immigrants had not moved in? Any adequate discussion of job displacement must include estimates of both of these factors, but none do. What is uncontested is that black migration out of the South—which began only after earlier waves of mass immigration ended prior to World War I—has been reversed during the 1980s, and for the first time in US history blacks now are moving into the South. As Raymond Frost (1991) finds, "there is a competitive relationship between immigration and black migration out of the South . . . [W]hen the rate of immigration declines, black migration to the North and West increases; when the rate of immigration increases, black migration declines" (p. 64). Black migration out of the South to the North and West fell during the 1970s to the lowest level (313,000) since the 1911–20 period, and it actually became negative (444,000) during the 1980s, with a net flow of blacks back to the South (Frost 1991, 64). [12]

Looked at from another perspective, no racial group since the nation won its independence received fewer new members as immigrants than the black population. When the nineteenth century began, blacks constituted about 20 percent of the US population; by the end of the century, the mass immigration of whites from Europe had reduced the black population to about 10 percent. As Passel and Edmonston (1992) observe, "almost the entire black population of the United States is descended from slaves who were forced to immigrate to the United States before the middle of the nineteenth century" (p. 8). As noted earlier, almost all of the post–1965 immigration to the United States has been comprised of people who presently constitute minority groups in the US population—but virtually all of these minority immigrants have been Hispanics and Asians. There have been relatively few blacks. Thus, one of the most dramatic effects of post–1965 immigration has been to create a significant shift in the makeup of the nation's minority population. As Passel and Edmonston (1992) write,

---

[12]   The migration data cited in Frost 1991 is for only nine years during the 1980s.

The proportion of the minority population [of the United States] that is black has been dropping steadily. This trend passed a little-noticed threshold in the 1990 Census. For the first time, the black population now accounts for less than half of the minority population. (p. 6)

Looking ahead to the twenty-first century, they state that "we can expect this shift to have profound implications for political and social relations among race/ethnic groups in the United States" (p. 6).

Under most circumstances, the fact that the racial and ethnic composition of the United States is changing would warrant neither concern nor policy changes to avoid such an outcome. But the economic welfare and the social status of blacks in the United States is a special case. The historical treatment of blacks as slaves in an otherwise free society, combined with the toleration of overt segregation in the region of the country where most blacks lived for another hundred years after the Civil War, has placed special obligations on succeeding generations of Americans to try to right the wrongs of the past. There may be legitimate disagreements among Americans over the extent to which such a correction can be achieved by public policy interventions (e.g., by affirmative action programs, anti-poverty programs, or remedial attention to education, housing, and health needs). But certainly there should be no disagreement over the normative principle that no discretionary element of public policy should be allowed to inflict harm upon black Americans in their quest for equality of opportunity. Unfortunately, post–1965 immigration policy has not been benign in its effect on blacks. It has been malignant. To be sure, this was not the goal of immigration reformers in the 1960s or of immigration supporters in the years since. But to allow the prevailing immigration system to continue to function without regard to its adverse effects on blacks can only lead to one conclusion: immigration policy has once more become a form of institutional racism. It has provided a way to avoid addressing the dire economic plight of black Americans.

6

Immigration Reform for the Next Century

As the end of the twentieth century approaches, the United States finds its labor market in a state of flux. There is a mismatch between the demand and supply of labor, and the future prospects are for this mismatch to worsen. Under such circumstances, all elements of public policy need to be accountable for the role they play in narrowing the gap between these two labor market determinants. The mounting concern over labor-force "preparedness," after all, is essentially a concern for the quality of labor. There is absolutely no evidence that the United States has labor shortages per se, but it does face the prospect of selected shortages of skilled and educated workers in specific geographic areas.

Furthermore, the United States is in the midst of a period of significant social change. The roles of women and minorities in the labor force are changing, not only with regard to their growing numbers, but also with respect to their aspirations about the types of jobs they seek. The prospects for domestic tranquility require that no element of public policy hamper this quest for inclusion in the labor force by native-born groups who previously have been excluded and underutilized. In this economic and social context, prevailing US immigration policy represents a major challenge to the future welfare of the American people in the twenty-first century. Immigration policy has become purely political and has been allowed to develop without any concern for its congruence with these labor-market trends. As a purely discretionary policy, the nation can ill afford to continue such counterproductive influences.

The issue does not revolve around immigrants themselves. They are merely responding to the opportunities that current immigration policy affords. Rather, the imperative is to change the direction and role of immigration policy so that all of its components serve the national interest and cease to threaten it.

The first step toward creation of a responsible policy is to establish the principle that the primary role of immigration into the United States should be to admit a limited number of workers who, in the short run, are needed to fill identifiable labor shortages and to restrict to a minimum the entry of those unqualified to fill such shortages. Spouses, minor children, and parents should continue to be allowed to accompany each visa-holder.

But an estimate of their numbers should be included in the annual number of entries to be allowed each year so that the total number of entries is capped. Adult family reunification and refugee accommodation should continue to be part of the overall system, but they should be clearly relegated to secondary levels of importance.

To accomplish this goal, Congress should establish an overall immigration ceiling, which should represent the sum of the maximum number of legal immigrants, refugees, and asylees permitted to enter the United States in a given year. The legislative ceiling should be seen as a maximum entry number; it should not be viewed as a goal to be achieved. Within the context of this legislative ceiling, the actual level of immigration for any given year should be set administratively by an agency of the executive branch. The number could range anywhere from zero up to the authorized annual ceiling. By permitting the annual number of admissions to be set administratively, there would be an element of flexibility added to the system which is currently absent. It would mean that immigration policy could respond to different short-run, macro-economic circumstances. For example, if unemployment levels were high or increasing, one would expect authorized immigration admissions to be set at low levels; conversely, if unemployment levels were low or decreasing, they would be increased. The ability to adjust immigration to comply with changing economic conditions is a key feature of the immigration systems of both Canada and Australia, and it is a commonsense attribute that should be part of immigration policy in the United States.

To avoid possible abuse in setting the annual entry levels, the administrative agency should be required to defend its decision each year at public hearings before the appropriate committees of Congress. But the decision should *not* be subject to political negotiation or change by Congress. The check of the executive agency's power would be the fact that if the agency's decisions cannot be defended in a credible manner, Congress always has the power to change the law.

The specific agency responsible for setting the annual immigration level and for administering all facets of immigration policy should be given an employment-driven mission. Since most immigrants must enter the labor force directly and because many of their accompanying immediate family members do so eventually, a government agency with an employment mission is best able to judge how many immigrants should be admitted annually. Such an agency also would be better equipped to enforce laws that apply to immigrants at the workplace (for example, employer sanctions or anti-discrimination protections).

Ideally, this administrative agency would be the body that is also accountable for major national human-resource-development efforts. In addition to its immigration duties, this agency would be responsible for education, training, labor-market information, and equal employment opportunity policies. At present, of course, there exists no such super-agency for human resource development. As a consequence, the next best option would be to return responsibility for immigration policy to the US Department of Labor, which, as noted above, housed the Immigration and Naturalization Service from its founding in 1914 until 1940. Being an employment-oriented agency, the Labor Department could best identify the specific occupational needs that immigration might be able to address. It is better qualified to debate how overall employment levels could accommodate specific numbers of new immigrants. Moreover, because it also has enforcement responsibilities for wage and hour violations, child labor laws, occupational health and safety laws, and migrant farmworker protections, the Labor Department could easily add enforcement of employer sanctions and anti-discrimination provisions to its present duties. In all of these situations, enforcement would have to be increased through the provision of additional funds and staff or no policy reforms would have any practical result.

There are multiple reasons why it is inappropriate for the US Department of Justice to administer immigration policy. To begin with, the Justice Department comprises a dozen or so major governmental divisions, all pleading for attention from the Attorney General. In this context, immigration matters tend to be neglected or relegated to a lower priority. Moreover, the Justice Department is the most politicized and politically sensitive of all federal agencies. It often chooses to pursue short-run, expedient solutions to controversial policy issues. Seldom has it manifest any interest for the economic consequences of immigration, nor has it ever seen fit to establish any ongoing research program to monitor the influences of immigration on the labor market or the overall economy. Moreover, the statistical data on immigration that it generates are primarily designed to meet administrative purposes rather than to serve analytical needs.

When immigration policy was shifted to the Justice Department in 1940, an ancillary consequence was that the Senate and House judiciary committees gained responsibility for formulating immigration policy and for overseeing immigration affairs. Traditionally, membership on these committees has been reserved almost exclusively for lawyers. The result is that immigration law in the United States is obsessively complex and procedurally protracted. Another result is that immigration lawyers and consultants have found a flourishing business—a "honey pot"—in the intricacies of immigration law. In this legalistic atmosphere, which typically focuses on individual situations, the broader economic considerations affecting the collective welfare of US society have become a distant concern.

Returning the Immigration and Naturalization Service to its former home in the Labor Department would be a major step forward toward the achievement of an immigration policy that is accountable for its economic effects. The Labor Department is far better equipped to understand labor-market issues and to design and administer an immigration policy targeted to meet specific labor-force needs. Such an administrative shift also would mean that the labor and human resource committees of Congress would regain oversight responsibilities for immigration matters. These committees usually comprise members who are more familiar with labor-market concepts, more sensitive to labor-force needs, and more aware of the labor-market institutions that protect workers and prepare citizens for employment.

The primary policy objective should be to establish a targeted immigration policy designed to admit people who can fill job vacancies for which qualified citizens and resident aliens are presently unavailable. At this juncture, this means jobs that require significant skill preparation and educational investment. The number of immigrants annually admitted, however, should always be far fewer than the number actually needed to fill such jobs—immigration should never be allowed to discourage citizen workers from investing in preparing themselves for vocations that are expanding or to allow governmental bodies to end support for the human-resource-development programs needed to prepare citizens for the types of jobs that are emerging. Because it takes time for would-be workers to acquire skills and education, immigration policy can be used on a short-run basis to target experienced immigrant workers for permanent settlement who already possess these abilities. But the preparedness (or lack thereof) of the domestic labor force is the fundamental economic issue confronting the United States in the early 1990s. Over the long haul, citizen workers must be prepared to qualify for the jobs in the industrial sectors that are growing.

Furthermore, legal entry should be restricted primarily to skilled and educated immigrants because the United States has an overabundance of unskilled and poorly prepared would-be workers. There is no current or prospective labor shortage; in the technology-driven and internationally competitive economic setting of the 1990s, no industrialized nation that in 1992 has 27 million functionally illiterate adults—as does the United States—need fear an imminent shortage of unskilled workers *(Scientific American,* November 1992, 44). Moreover, if only to make matters worse, immigration—especially by illegal immigrants, amnesty recipients, and refugees—has itself become a major contributor to the growth of adult illiteracy in the United States *(Daily Labor Report,* 2 August 1985, A10). To this degree, by adding to the surplus of illiterate adult job-seekers, immigration serves to diminish the limited opportunities for poorly prepared citizens to find jobs or to improve their employability by on-the-job training. The nature and magnitude of immigration and refugee flows also contributes to the need to expand significantly public funding for remedial education, basic training, and English-literacy programs in many of the urban communities that have been impacted by their arrival. As the mayor of Washington, DC, Sharon Pratt Kelly, forcefully testified at a public hearing on the causes of a two-day riot in a largely immigrant section of that city in 1991:

> The frustrations have been festering for 12 years because federal policy has forced immigration into this area with no programs to accommodate this thrust and no dollars for education or jobs or social services. We have become a repository but no beneficiary of federal actions. *(Washington Post,* 30 January 1992, B1)

Too often, scarce local public funds are diverted away from upgrading the human-resource capabilities of the citizen and resident-alien labor force at a time when such endeavors should be the nation's number one domestic spending priority.

In addition to the high incidence of adult illiteracy, there should be no fear about any future shortage of unskilled workers for as long as the nation's educational system is experiencing a national high school dropout rate of 25 percent, a dropout rate of 40 percent for blacks, and a rate of over 50 percent for Hispanics (the two most rapidly growing groups in the youth population), and as long as the quality of education provided to many of these minority students who do graduate from high school "does not even meet the standard of a rising tide of mediocrity" (US Congress, Joint Economic Committee 1988, 1, 16).

Furthermore, it is important to note that the decline in the number of young people in the labor force that began in the 1980s is just about over. Beginning in 1996, young people will begin to increase again in absolute numbers so that, by 2005, this group is projected to be larger by about 2.8 million people than it was in 1990 (Kutscher 1991, 6). Thus, as the US Department of Labor has reported, "the worry about lack of entry level workers, which was of consequence in the late 1980s and early 1990s, should ease considerably, if not disappear entirely, as we progress through this decade [the 1990s]" (Kutscher 1991, 6).

A shift in admission preference away from the nepotistic principle of adult family reunification, which has dominated US immigration policy since 1965, and toward an employment-based admission system can be expected to engender fierce opposition. As an eminent authority on immigration, John Higham (1990–91) writes:

> This [the elimination of family preference] will be as difficult to change as were the earlier anomalies and deficiencies in American immigration policy. Like those earlier deficiencies, the family preference scheme will have a stubborn constituency in the ethnic groups that believe they benefit from it. Just as the national origin quotas suppressed variety in the alleged interests of the older American population, so the current law does the same in the supposed interest of the groups that have recently dominated the incoming stream. (p. 64)

In this same vein, it should be recalled that the rationale for establishing the priority for family reunification in 1965 was anything but noble in its original intentions. An immigration policy for the twenty-first century cannot continue to be predicated on the need to mollify the selfish political interests of certain ethnic and political groups. The goal must be to create a policy that serves the national interest. Thus, the most obvious component of the family reunification system that should be immediately eliminated is the preference category for adult brothers and sisters of US citizens. Under the Immigration Act of 1990, this specific preference category is given 65,000 visas a year (a slight increase over what the allocation had been since 1965). No other major immigrant-receiving nation in the world provides such an admission category. Indeed, earlier immigration reform efforts in the early 1980s called for the total elimination of this category, but the proposals did not survive the subsequent political deliberations. If adult brothers and sisters of US immigrants wish to immigrate to the United States, they should be required to qualify on the same grounds as other would-be immigrants. The other three family-related categories of the present system (see table 4) should be reduced significantly so as to total no more than 20 percent of the visas available each year.

Already having an abundance of unskilled or poorly educated adults, the last thing the nation needs as it enters the twenty-first century is to continue to allow unskilled and poorly educated persons to immigrate. It is always possible for more highly skilled and educated persons to perform unskilled work. Hence, in the unlikely case that all of the experts on labor-force trends and projections are wrong and the demand for unskilled workers grows and the need for skilled workers contracts, the operation of normal market forces should be able to guide the excess supply of skilled workers to fill vacant unskilled jobs. This assumes, of course, that the operation of the market is not sabotaged by an immigration policy designed to admit unskilled non-immigrant workers and that it will not continue to tolerate massive illegal entry of unskilled workers. But the reverse is not possible: if skilled and educated workers are needed, they cannot readily be created. Unskilled workers cannot fill skilled jobs except at great financial cost and significant time delays for retraining and relocation or with significant productivity losses for the economy due to inefficient operations. Moreover, the lack of sufficient educational foundations will prevent many currently unskilled adults from ever being trained for the types of jobs that are projected to be most in demand in the next decade.

Immigration can be used as a means of providing the types of experienced workers that are actually needed. Under present circumstances, these workers are those that already have skills and education and, for whatever reason, voluntarily wish to leave their homelands. Such is especially the case of workers who are in fields related to computer technology, scientific research, and higher education. In this capacity, immigration can find a justifiable purpose in this new era. Immigration policy can serve as a short-run method to fill these types of jobs until the nation can enact the quality ·human-resource-development policies capable of meeting this emerging domestic demand.

Largely by means of circumvention, the current immigration system is trying to perform this function despite the self-defeating burdens imposed on it. The non-immigrant system is becoming a significant avenue into the country's labor market for skilled and educated workers. The policy toward non-immigrants is supposed to allow for the admission of foreign workers to fill temporary spot shortages. Eventually, the non-immigrants are expected to return to their homelands and, over time, market forces combined with public and private training should generate a domestic labor supply to fill such jobs. It is not intended to be an avenue for permanent immigration or a means of long-term worker dependency by US employers. However, because the preponderance of available visas are restricted to family-related admissions and because in the past there have been lengthy backlogs of applicants or country ceilings that have affected the availability of the employment-based visas, many employers have turned to non-immigrants to find experienced workers without having to compete, hire, or train from within the native-born pool. There are no annual ceilings for most of the relevant non-immigrant categories, and some workers are permitted to remain in the country for many years. As matters now stand, it is conceivable that non-immigrant workers could soon become as or more important than the existing legal immigrant system in terms of the implications for the US labor supply. This is, of course, a perversion of immigration policy. The adoption of an employment-based legal immigration system should mean a sharp contraction in the usage of non-immigrant workers, and such an objective should be explicitly included in any new immigration statute.

A shift from a family-based to a labor-market-oriented immigration policy, of course, does have its dangers. The use of immigration as a source of experienced workers should be viewed as a policy of last resort; it should be used only in consort with other public policy measures intended to develop the employment potential of the nation's human resources. Labor shortages, as they develop, should not be viewed as a problem to be solved only by immigration. Rather, labor shortages should be viewed as an opportunity to educate youth, to retrain adults, to eliminate discriminatory barriers, and to introduce voluntary relocation programs to assist would-be workers to move from areas of labor surplus to areas of labor shortage. Only then should the administrative agency responsible for setting the annual immigration level and the occupational needs permit immigration to occur.

As matters now stand, the incidence of unemployment, poverty, and adult illiteracy is much higher and the educational attainment levels significantly lower for blacks and Hispanics than for non-Hispanic whites and most Asians. In addition, blacks and Hispanics are disproportionately employed in industries and occupations already in sharpest decline—goods-producing industries and blue-collar occupations. Thus, the most rapidly increasing groups in the labor force are precisely those most at risk from the changing employment requirements. Unless public policy measures are targeted to their human-resource-development needs, many members of minority groups, as well as other vulnerable segments of the general population, will have dim employment and income prospects in the twenty-first century. The United States cannot allow its labor force to continue to polarize along racial and class lines if it hopes to prosper and to enjoy any semblance of domestic tranquility. If the current policy of mass and unguided immigration continues, it is unlikely that there will be sufficient political pressure to enact the long-term human-resource-development policies needed to prepare and to incorporate these segments of the population into the mainstream economy. Instead, by providing both competition and alternatives, the large and unplanned influx of immigrant labor will serve to maintain the social marginalization of many citizen blacks and citizen Hispanics. It will also mean that job opportunities will be reduced for the growing numbers of older workers who may wish to prolong their working years and for the vast pool of disabled citizens who, with the aid of the Americans with Disabilities Act of 1990, are seeking access to employment opportunities. In other words, a substantial human reserve of potential citizen workers already exists. If their human-resource-development needs were addressed comprehensively, they could provide an ample supply of workers for most of the foreseeable labor-force needs of the early twenty-first century.

It goes without saying that an employment-based immigration system is predicated on the assumption that every effort be made to reduce illegal immigration. It is probably impossible in a free society to stop illegal immigration entirely, but the goal should be to actively pursue every possible means to reduce its incidence. The presumption that the nation should have an employment-based immigration policy is anchored on the notion that its terms can be enforced. In the past, illegal immigration has undermined the credibility of whatever immigration system has been in place. It continues to do so. This chronic violation of public policy cannot be permitted to continue. Hence, an immigration policy for the twenty-first century must contain strong provisions for enforcement of its terms. Employer sanctions must remain the core of the deterrence against illegal immigration, but the current loopholes with regard to the use of fraudulent documents and the absence of a counterfeit proof identification system must be corrected. Also, financial penalties should be imposed on illegal immigrants themselves, just as they are on other federal offenders. Additional funds and staff should be devoted to border enforcement activities and inland investigations of "visa overstayers" by the Immigration and Naturalization Service. Stronger physical barriers may need to be constructed at those points along the border where massive illegal entry is known to occur. State and local government agencies responsible for enforcing labor statutes should be empowered and obligated to assist the INS in enforcement. More attention should be paid to addressing the "push" factors in the major source countries: forms of assistance should be tailored to the particular factors in those countries that cause so many of their citizens to leave their homelands. These pressures may involve such concerns as excessive population pressures, mass poverty, government corruption, or widespread human rights violations. US assistance could take the form of family planning assistance, limited trade concessions, economic development assistance, technical assistance, and linkages of aid programs to strict adherence to human rights protections. But the bottom line must be that illegal immigration to the United States is no longer a viable option.

The issue of accommodating refugees and asylees, of course, will be more complicated to address in an immigration system based on economic needs. Certainly the United States is obligated to participate in worldwide efforts to assist legitimate political refugees. Refugee admission should be considered an exception to the general rules for immigration, but there still must be restrictions on refugee levels that enable there to be control on overall immigration. Options other than settlement in the United States should be given at least equal weight. Aside from efforts to resettle refugees in other countries near their homelands when feasible or to provide financial aid to support refugees in camps while they remain in neighboring countries (if conditions in their homelands are expected to improve in the near future), the United States should link its foreign aid and foreign trade policies to adherence to human rights principles in those countries that generate mass numbers of political refugees. Nonetheless, when there is no other recourse, those refugees and their family members who have sustained persecution for their individual actions should be admitted on a limited basis. The President should, as now, set a goal for annual refugee admissions that reflects his assessment of expected world developments. This number would be included in the aforementioned annual immigration figure. If the number is less than 50,000 per year (the figure that was originally considered to be "normal" when the Refugee Act of 1980 became law), all could be admitted. If the number exceeds that level, there should be a one-for-one reduction in the number of family-related visas available for that year. If the nation is ever to gain a semblance of control over its immigration system, there must be a check on the number of refugees admitted each year. This will require a conscious decision. There must be some "tradeoff." A legal link between the legal immigration flow and refugee flow must be reestablished (as was the case from 1965 to 1980). Otherwise, the political temptation is, as has been the case, for the federal government to act in a piecemeal fashion that often makes a mockery of any effort to establish a coherent immigration policy, with local and state governments often bearing most of the subsequent costs associated with refugee accommodation. Indeed, because refugees are admitted to the United States as a direct result of federal policy decisions, it would be preferable for the federal government to absorb all of the financial costs associated with preparing refugees for employment and settling families in communities.

The issue of political asylees raises the same questions as refugees. There must be an expedited method to separate legitimate claims for political asylum from claims by people who simply seek a pretext to enter the country for personal economic gain. Past efforts to address this issue have included proposals to limit the right to appeal negative decisions of asylee adjudication to those stemming from procedural errors; substantive rulings on the merits of such decisions would not be appealable. These provisions were bitterly opposed by immigration lawyers and by some civil rights organizations, but the current system of lengthy appeals, protracted cases, and high legal costs simply cannot be sustained. A way of bringing these cases to rapid closure must be found. The Asylum Officer Corps, established in 1990, which has officials specially trained for these purposes, should be empowered by limiting appeal of their negative decisions to procedural violations alone. Likewise, if such expedited decision-making procedures could be established, the practice of keeping asylee applicants in detention while their cases are resolved could be applied uniformly. Otherwise, one is confronted with the present mockery, where many applicants simply make an asylum request, are released on their own recognizance, and disappear into the illegal immigrant pool before their adjudication hearing is held (or soon after a hearing in which their application was denied).

The United States needs to adopt an immigration policy that is consistent with the rapidly changing economic and social trends that are restructuring the US labor force and society. If congruent with these trends, immigration policy can provide a valuable tool to help enhance economic efficiency and achieve societal equity. If contradictory to these trends, immigration policy can present a major barrier to the accomplishment of either or both goals. The luxury of allowing immigration policy to continue to be determined on purely political criteria (i.e., to placate special interest groups) and to achieve social engineering goals (i.e., to pursue diversity simply for its own sake) can ill be afforded. Making immigration policy a human-resource-development policy would give immigration policy what it now lacks and what the nation desperately needs: accountability and credibility.

References

Bailey, Thomas R. 1987. *Immigrant and Native Workers: Contrasts and Competition.* Boulder, CO: Westview Press.

Barringer, Felicity. 1991. "Census Shows Profound Change in Racial Makeup of the Nation," *New York Times* (11 March).

Bishop, John H., and Shani Carter. 1991. "How Accurate Are Recent BLS Occupational Projections?" *Monthly Labor Review* (October).

Bogen, Elizabeth. 1987. *Immigration in New York.* New York: Praeger Publishers.

Borjas, George, and Stephen J. Trejo. 1991. "Immigrant Participation in the Welfare System," *Industrial and Labor Relations Review* (January), 195–211.

Borjas, George. 1990. *Friends or Strangers? The Impact of Immigration on the US Economy.* New York: Basic Books.

Bound, John, and George Johnson. 1992. "Changes in the Structure of Wages in the 1980s: An Evaluation of Alternative Explanations," *American Economic Review* (June), 371–92.

Bouvier, Leon F., and Vernon M. Briggs, Jr. 1988. *The Population and Labor Force of New York: 1990 to 2050.* Washington, DC: Population Reference Bureau.

Bouvier, Leon, and Bob Weller. 1992. *Florida in the 21st Century.* Washington, DC: Center for Immigration Studies.

Bouvier, Leon F. 1991a. *Fifty Million Californians.* Washington, DC: Center for Immigration Studies.

————. 1991b. *Peaceful Invasions: Immigration and Changing America.* Washington, DC: Center for Immigration Studies.

————. 1986. *Population Change and the Future of Texas.* Washington, DC: Population Reference Bureau.

Briggs, Vernon M., Jr. 1992. *Mass Immigration and the National Interest.* Armonk, NY: M. E. Sharpe.

————. 1984. *Immigration Policy and the American Labor Force.* Baltimore: Johns Hopkins University Press.

Brock, William E., US Secretary of Labor. 1987. Address to the National Press Club, Washington, DC (5 March). Mimeo.

Card, David. 1990. "The Impact of the Mariel Boatlift on the Miami Labor Market," *Industrial and Labor Relations Review* (January), 245–57.

Chiswick, Barry. 1986. "Is the New Immigration Less Skilled than the Old?" *Journal of Labor Economics* (April), 192–96.

Commission on Workforce Quality and Labor Market Efficiency. 1989. *Investing in People: A Strategy to Address America's Workforce Crisis.* Washington, DC: US Department of Labor.

Cyert, Richard M., and David C. Mowry. 1987. *Technology and Employment.* Washington, DC: National Academy Press.

Fix, Michael, and Jeffrey S. Passel. 1991. *The Door Remains Open: Recent Immigration to the United States and a Preliminary Analysis of the Immigration Act of 1990.* Washington, DC: Urban Institute.

Frost, Raymond M. 1991. "Blacks and Immigration," *Challenge: The Magazine of Economic Affairs* (November-December).

Fullerton, Howard N., Jr. 1989. "New Labor Force Projections Spanning 1988 to 2000," *Monthly Labor Review* (November), 2–12.

Hayghe, Howard V. 1990. "Family Members in the Work Force," *Monthly Labor Review* (March).

Higham, John. 1990–91. "The Purpose of Legal Immigration in the 1990s and Beyond," *Social Contract* (Winter).

Killingsworth, Charles C. 1978. "The Fall and Rise of the Idea of Structural Unemployment," Presidential Address, *Proceedings of the 31st Meeting of the Industrial Relations Research Association.* Madison, WI: Industrial Relations Research Association.

Kletzer, Lori G. 1991. "Job Displacement, 1979–86: How Blacks Fared Relative to Whites," *Monthly Labor Review* (July).

Kutscher, Ronald E. 1991. "New BLS Projections: Findings and Implications," *Monthly Labor Review* (November).

Lebergott, Stanley. 1964. *Manpower in Economic Growth.* New York: McGraw-Hill.

Marshall, Ray. 1988. "Immigration in the Golden State: The Tarnished Dream," in *US Immigration in the 1980s: Reappraisal and Reform,* edited by David E. Simcox. Boulder, CO: Westview Press.

McCarthy, Kevin, and R. Burciago Valdez. 1985. *Current and Future Effects of Mexican Immigration in California: Executive Summary.* Santa Monica, CA: RAND Corporation.

Miles, Jack. 1992. "Immigration and the New American Dilemma: Blacks vs. Browns," *Atlantic Monthly* (October), 41–68.

Mines, Richard, and Jeffrey Avina. 1992. "Immigrants and Labor Standards: The Case of California Janitors," in *US Mexico Relations: Labor Market Interdependence,* edited by Jorge A. Bustamante et al. Stanford, CA: Stanford University Press, 429–48.

Mines, Richard, and Philip Martin. 1984. "Immigrant Workers and the California Citrus Industry," *Industrial Relations* (Spring).

Muller, Thomas, and Thomas J. Espenshade. 1985. *The Fourth Wave: California's Newest Immigrants.* Washington, DC: Urban Institute.

National Research Council, Panel on Immigration Statistics. 1985. *Immigration Statistics: A Story of Neglect.* Washington, DC: US Government Printing Office.

North, David S., and Marion F. Houstoun. 1976. *The Characteristics and Role of Illegal Aliens in the US Labor Market: An Exploratory Study.* Washington, DC: Linton and Company.

Oxford Analytica. 1986. *America in Perspective.* Boston: Houghton-Mifflin.

Passel, Jeffrey S., and Barry Edmonston. 1992. *Immigration and Race in the United States: The 20th and 21st Centuries,* PRIP–UI–20. Washington, DC: Urban Institute, Program for Research on Immigration Policy.

Pear, Robert. 1991. "Bigger Number of New Mothers Are Unmarried," *New York Times* (4 December), A20.

———. 1992. "New Look at the US in 2050: Bigger, Older, and Less White," *New York Times* (12 December), A1, D18.

Personick, Valerie. 1987. "Industry Output and Employment through the End of the Century," *Monthly Labor Review* (September), 30–45.

Reinhold, Robert. 1992. "A Terrible Chain of Events Reveal Los Angeles without Its Makeup," *New York Times* (3 May), E1.

Roberts, Peter. 1913. *The New Immigration.* New York: Macmillan.

Rones, Philip L. 1986. "An Analysis of Regional Employment Growth, 1973–85," *Monthly Labor Review* (July), 3–13.

SCIRP. *See* Select Commission on Immigration and Refugee Policy.

Select Commission on Immigration and Refugee Policy. 1981. *US Immigration Policy and the National Interest.* Washington, DC: US Government Printing Office (March).

Silvestri, George T., and John M. Lukasiewicz. 1987. "A Look at Occupational Employment Trends to the Year 2000," *Monthly Labor Review* (September), 46–63.

Taylor, Paul. 1991. "Nonmarital Births: As Rates Soar, Theories Abound," *Washington Post* (22 January), A3.

Thurow, Lester. 1992. *Head to Head: The Coming Economic Battle among Japan, Europe, and America.* New York: William Morrow.

Tienda, Marta, et al. 1991. *The Demography of Legalization: Insights from Administrative Records of Legalized Aliens: Final Report.* Chicago: University of Chicago, Population Research Center.

Uchitelle, Louis. 1987. "America's Army of Non-Workers," *New York Times* (17 September), F1, F6.

US Congress. 1964. House. Subcommittee No. 1 of the Committee on the Judiciary. "Testimony of Robert F. Kennedy, US Attorney General," *Hearings.* 88th Cong., 2d sess.

US Congress, Joint Economic Committee. 1988. "The Education Deficit," *Staff Report Summarizing the Hearings on Competitiveness and the Quality of the American Labor Force.* Washington, DC: US Government Printing Office.

US Coordinator for Refugee Affairs. 1992. *Proposed Refugee Admissions for Fiscal Year 1993: Report to Congress.* Washington, DC: US Department of State.

US Department of State. 1965. "Statement by Secretary of State Dean Rusk before the Subcommittee on Immigration of the US Senate Committee on the Judiciary," in "Department Urges Congress to Revise Immigration Laws," *Department of State Bulletin* (24 August).

US Immigration Commission. 1911. *Abstracts of the Reports of the US Immigration Commission,* volume 1. Washington, DC: US Government Printing Office.

Van Arsdol, Maurice D., et al. 1979. *Non-Apprehended and Apprehended Undocumented Residents in the Los Angeles Labor Market.* Report prepared for the US Department of Labor, Employment and Training Administration (contract no. 20-06-77-16) (May).

Vobejda, Barbara. 1991a. "Half of Population Lives in Urban Areas," *Washington Post* (21 February), A1, A12.

————. 1991b. "25% of Black Women May Never Marry," *Washington Post* (11 November), A1, A12.

Washington, Booker T. 1895. "The Atlanta Exposition Address," *Up from Slavery.* Reprinted in *Three Negro Classics.* New York: Avon Books, 1965.

Wilson, William Julius. 1987. *The Truly Disadvantaged: The Inner City, the Underclass, and Public Policy.* Chicago: University of Chicago Press.

Part Two

The Economic Case for More Immigrants

Stephen Moore

1

Introduction

Many decades ago, prize-winning author Oscar Handlin wrote that he "once thought to write a history of immigration. Then I discovered that immigrants *are* American history" (Handlin 1951). That the United States today is a nation of immigrants is not just a tired and worn-out cliché. No other country on earth has brought together so many people from so many diverse nations and then successfully integrated them into one society.

The statistics on immigration to the United States are awe-inspiring. In this century, some fifty million immigrants have come—one of the largest migrations of people ever. In the 1980s alone, nearly eight million newcomers arrived to these shores, some as skill-based and family-based legal immigrants, some as refugees fleeing persecution from abroad, and some as illegal aliens—almost all of them in a quest to find freedom and economic opportunity. According to the 1990 census, roughly one in twelve residents of the United States was born abroad. In some states, such as California, Florida, and Texas, nearly one in four residents is an immigrant. It is estimated that there are more people of Polish descent living in the United States than in Poland.

Few Americans would dispute that this large migration of freedom-seekers has been a net asset to the United States economy in this century. What is disputed is whether continuing immigration at current or even expanded levels is in the national interest. Many of today's economic ills are said to be intensified by the new immigrants, especially those from less developed countries (Lamm and Imhoff 1986). Some opponents of immigration have suggested that although immigrants served a vital purpose in helping build the United States in its early stages of economic development, more people are neither necessary nor desirable as America enters a stage of economic maturity (Briggs 1992).

Immigrants are certainly not an unmixed blessing. When the newcomers first arrive, they impose short-term costs on the citizenry. Because immigration means more people, they cause more congestion on our highways, a more crowded housing market, and longer waiting lines in stores and hospitals. In states such as California, immigrants' children are heavy users of an already overburdened public school system, and so on. Some immigrants abuse the welfare system, which means that tax dollars from Americans are transferred to immigrant populations. Los Angeles County officials estimate that immigrants' use of county services costs the local government hundreds of millions of dollars each year. It is also true that in many occupations and local labor markets, newly arriving immigrants intensify competition for jobs. And the very fact that large immigration brings about economic and social change—even when that change might be economically constructive—is often unwelcome for many US–born citizens who are nostalgic for "the good old days."

The benefits of immigration, however, are manifold. Perhaps the most important benefit is that immigrants come to the United States with critically needed talents, energies, and ambitions that serve as an engine for economic progress and help the United States retain economic and geopolitical leadership. Because for most of the world's immigrants, America is their first choice, the United States is in a unique position within the industrialized world to select the most brilliant and inventive minds from the United Kingdom, Canada, China, Korea, India, Ireland, Mexico, Philippines, Russia, Taiwan, and other nations. Because most immigrants are not poor, tired, huddled masses, but rather are above the average of their compatriots in skill and education levels, the immigration process has a highly beneficial self-selection component, a skimming of the cream of the best workers and top brainpower from the rest of the world (Gibney 1990). In short, the importation of human capital through immigration is perhaps America's premier comparative advantage in a global economy today.

Immigrants are not just additional people; they are people with uniquely developed skills, talents, and cultural backgrounds. Their diversity is an unqualified benefit to the United States: it helps cultivate new knowledge-creation and technological innovation. Their unique skills allow America to fill those niches in the labor market that cannot be filled by US–born citizens. Immigrants are not just productive themselves, they also make US–born citizens more productive.

An equally critical advantage of immigration to the United States is that it is a continuous process of national rebirth and rejuvenation of the American spirit of enterprise. This is no small advantage. More than perhaps any other single national policy, the continued admission of enterprising new immigrants safeguards the United States from economic and geopolitical decline—the kind of evolutionary decline that has been the fate of so many other powerful and prosperous empires of the past. "What gives resonance to our republic," noted former U.N. Ambassador Jeane Kirkpatrick at the hundredth anniversary of the Statue of Liberty, "is its continual renewal by new citizens who bring to us a special sense of the importance of freedom and liberty" (Kirkpatrick 1986).

Specifically, the most critical economic benefits from immigration are:

- Immigrants are highly entrepreneurial. Their rate of business start-ups and self-employment tend to be higher than that of US–born citizens. Most immigrant enterprises are small and not unusually profitable. But others, such as Wang Computers, founded in Seattle by an Asian immigrant, are Fortune 500 firms employing thousands of US workers.

- Immigrants contribute to the global competitiveness of US corporations, particularly in high-technology industries. Tens of thousands of exceptionally talented scientists and engineers are preserving the global leadership of US firms in frontier industries such as biotechnology, robotics, computers, electronics, semiconductors, and pharmaceuticals. Silicon Valley is the modern-day American melting pot.

- Many US industries are highly dependent on the flow of hard-working, low-skilled immigrant labor. These include the fruit and vegetable, apparel and garment, poultry, and restaurant industries, among others. Without an influx of immigrant labor, many of these industries would close down or move their operations overseas—meaning fewer jobs for American workers and a weakening of our international trade balances. Indeed, the *Wall Street Journal* has described low-skilled immigrants as "the backbone of the California economy."

- The children of immigrants tend to be highly successful professionals with very high education levels and earnings. A very high percentage of high-school valedictorians, Westinghouse Science Contest award winners, Spelling Bee champions, and National Merit Scholars are immigrants or the children of immigrants. Immigrant children tend to have higher earnings than US–born workers, and they tend to be highly represented in professional occupations. America's corporate and political leaders of tomorrow are the children of today's immigrants.

- Most important, immigrants increase the aggregate income of US–born citizens and thereby increase US economic growth. Studies show that the net effect of immigrants—even low-skilled immigrants—is to raise the overall productivity level of US citizens. The long-term impact of immigration is higher economic growth and higher living standards for US citizens.

Opponents of immigration maintain that the economic costs of a generous immigration policy outweigh these benefits. However, research shows that almost all of the major objections to continued immigration are exaggerated. In fact, a careful review of the evidence on the economic impact of immigration leads to the following conclusions:

1) Immigrants use welfare and other social services at about the same rate that US–born citizens do. The taxes paid by immigrants typically cover the cost of public services they use.

2) The newest immigrants—particularly Asians—are not less skilled or less educated than previous waves of immigrants, and they may be even more skilled and entrepreneurial than immigrants of the past. There is no evidence to suggest that we are at a historic turning point with respect to the benefits of immigration.

3) There is no evidence to support the claim that over the long term immigrants cause unemployment or depress wages of US citizens. Immigrants create at least as many jobs as they take by expanding the size of the economy.

4) The United States is not being overpopulated by immigrants, and immigration is not at a historically unprecedented level today. The United States is capable of absorbing well over a million immigrants per year without overwhelming our physical and social infrastructure.

5) The impact of immigrants on heavily impacted cities is almost uniformly positive. Immigrants have prevented a catastrophic decline in the population and thus the tax base of large cities; they have revived declining inner city areas; and have started tens of thousands of new business enterprises in urban America.

Let us review each of these claims individually, then discuss in detail how immigrants benefit the US economy, and finally, suggest reforms to the immigration laws that may multiply these benefits.

2

The Demographic Impact of Immigrants

There is an apocryphal story of a German immigrant who, after taking the oath of United States citizenship, was asked how it felt to be an American. Without skipping a beat, the man responded with his thick German accent, "I suddenly feel a rising tide of resentment against all these foreigners coming to these shores."

Most Americans have come to believe that the United States is accepting unprecedented numbers of immigrants—that the nation is virtually "under siege" from foreigners. Many of our politicians have tried to reinforce this sense of an out-of-control border by resorting in some cases to frightening rhetoric. Former presidential candidate Patrick Buchanan (1990) spoke of the need to "build a sea wall around the United States" to keep out "the rising masses of foreigners." Former Colorado Governor Richard Lamm (1986) warns that the millions of legal and illegal immigrants coming to these shores are causing a "cultural contamination."

The truth is that there is very little validity to such hysteria. It is indeed true that immigration reached very high levels in the 1980s: nearly eight million legal immigrants arrived from 1980 to 1990, roughly one million as refugees, one million as job-related immigrants, and six million family-based immigrants. This is the highest number of immigrants to come to the United States in any decade except the great wave that arrived through Ellis Island between 1900 and 1910.

For selected regions of the country, this represented a substantial flow of new people to be integrated into the economy. Roughly half of all immigrants settled in just four states: California, Florida, Texas, and Illinois.

Opponents of immigration often charge that immigrants are causing an overpopulation problem in the United States. Some environmental groups maintain that America's policy should be population stabilization and that immigration impedes this goal. However, if overpopulation is measured by the number of people per square mile, then the United States is one of the most underpopulated industrialized nations in the world. Moreover, there is no economic or environmental rationale why population stabilization is preferable to a growth rate of 1, 2, or 3 percent. Most of the recent economic research has come to dismiss the argument that population growth is in any way inimical to economic growth or sound environmental policy (J. Simon 1981; J. Simon and Moore 1989). In fact, there is substantial evidence that moderate positive population expansion is more consistent with economic growth than zero growth or negative growth (J. Simon 1981).

But let us accept for a moment the proposition that rapid population growth is harmful, and that this is a worry for America. The anti-population groups frequently back their assertion that immigration is causing too-rapid growth with statistics that show that over the past decade immigrants have accounted for a much larger share of US population growth than ever before. Yet this is an extremely slippery, if not deceptive, statistic. For example, if a nation had zero population growth among its native-born population over a given period and then allowed the admission of even one immigrant, immigration would account for 100 percent of population growth. But that would prove little about the real impact of immigration.

In fact, the reason immigration accounts for a high rate of population growth is precisely because the US birth rate declined in the 1970s and 1980s and now remains very near the replacement rate (Wattenberg 1985). If our concern is overpopulation, the fact that US–born citizens are having fewer children is not an argument for less immigration; if anything, it is an argument that America can easily absorb *more* immigrants without risking a population explosion.

One thing is certain: even with substantially higher immigration than today, America is not on the brink of a population explosion. In the 1980s, despite eight million new immigrants, population growth was lower than during any decade since the wartime 1940s. Two years ago, I examined the demographic impact of various levels of immigration over the decade of the 1990s (Moore 1990c). The upper-bound estimate of immigration levels analyzed was ten million over the decade. Would such an immigrant flow contribute to a skyrocketing population in the United States? The answer, as shown in figure 1, is clearly no. Even assuming this unlikely upper limit of immigration, the population growth rate in the 1990s would be only about half the level of the 1950s. Most demographers predict that population growth will remain low during the first few decades of the next century, because of lower birth rates and the aging of the baby boom generation (Wattenberg 1985). Hence, there is little reason to restrain immigration to the United States because of population worries.

Another demographic factor that will mitigate the burden of absorbing immigrants in the 1990s is the very slow growth expected in the labor force. Table 1 shows that even if immigration were to increase to about one million entrants per year for the rest of the decade, the US labor force would increase at half the pace of the 1970s. This does not appear to be a great cause for worry.

Perhaps the best measure of America's ability to absorb immigrants into the social and physical infrastructure is the number of immigrants admitted as a share of the total population. To see why, consider two cities, one of 1,000 people and one of 100,000 people. Now assume that 1,000 immigrants enter each city. In the city of 1,000, the immigrants will double the population, causing all sorts of short-term problems—shortages of housing, office space, parking, and maybe even food; a burden on schools; long lines at stores; intense competition for jobs; and an immense impact on the culture of the city, among others. But in the city of 100,000 people, an increase of 1,000 immigrants would be virtually unnoticed. The immigrants would be absorbed very quickly into the job market and the existing social institutions. This is why it is important to know how many immigrants enter the United States relative to the number of people already here, which is the immigration rate.

The US immigration rate has risen from about 2.0 per 1,000 residents in the 1950s and 1960s to about 3.2 per 1,000 residents in the 1980s. This is not cause for great concern, however. As figure 2 illustrates, in earlier periods of our history, the immigration rate has been as high as 16 per 1,000—five times higher than today. The average immigration rate over the past 150 years has been about 5 per 1,000 residents. To reach this rate, the United States would have to open its doors to about 1.3 million immigrants per year; as figure 2 shows, the immigration rate in this decade will be less than 3.5 per 1,000. This is not a terribly troubling prospect.

Today, more than twenty million Americans—or more than one in twelve US residents—is foreign-born. This is a fairly large increase from the 1950s and 1960s, when one in twenty Americans was foreign-born. In early periods, as many as one in six Americans was foreign-born: we were much more a nation

Figure 1. Population Growth by Decade

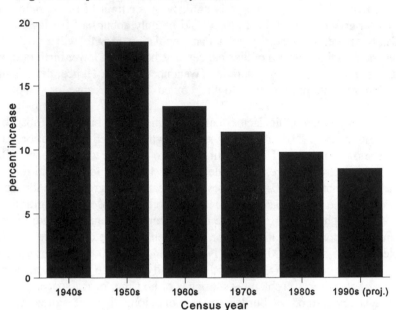

Source: Bureau of the Census, *Statistical Abstract of the United States, 1992.*
Washington, DC: US Department of Commerce, p. 8; projections by author.

of immigrants a century ago than we are today (see figure 3). The argument is
made by immigration critics that at the turn of the century, America was a young,
underdeveloped nation that needed strong bodies; in the 1990s we need strong
minds. But as I will document below, we need strong minds *and* strong bodies
today, and immigration is continuously providing us with both.

Immigration critics often suggest that American immigration policy is
overly generous by arguing that the United States has opened its doors to more
immigrants and refugees than the rest of the world combined. But comparing
the number of immigrants entering each industrialized country relative to its
overall population, we see that the United States no longer appears overly
generous in distributing visas. Of the three major immigrant-receiving countries—Australia, Canada, and the United States—the United States has the
lowest immigration rate. In 1985, the United States allowed entry to 3 immigrants
per 1,000 population, Australia 12, and Canada 3.5. Even Denmark (6 per

Table 1. Growth of US Labor Force by Decade, 1940–2000*

	Labor Force at End of Decade (Millions)	Increase in Labor Force (Millions)	Percentage Increase in Labor Force
1940–1950	62.2	9.5	18
1950–1960	69.6	7.4	12
1960–1970	82.8	13.2	19
1970–1980	106.9	24.1	29
1980–1990	124.9	18.0	17
1990–2000	143.5	18.6	15

*   Assumes ten million immigrants (one million per year) between 1991 and
2000, and a labor-force participation rate for immigrants of 70 percent.

Source: William B. Johnston and Arnold Packer, *Workforce 2000.* Indianapolis:
Hudson Institute, 1987, and calculations by author.

1,000), Germany (7 per 1,000), Switzerland (15 per 1,000), and the United
Kingdom (4 per 1,000) had more immigrants as a share of resident population
than the United States (Council of Europe 1986). The economic evidence for
Australia, Canada, and the United Kingdom indicates that immigration to these
countries has had a mostly positive impact on growth rates (J. Simon 1990).

An issue of mounting concern for many Americans and some policymakers
is the ethnic composition of the "new immigrants." Nineteen-ninety-two
presidential candidate Patrick Buchanan (1990) has insisted that America is
losing its "white European culture." In a highly publicized cover story of the
National Review, Peter Brimelow (1992) voices concern over the growing tide
of non-European immigration. A prediction by demographers that by 2050
whites in Texas would be a minority received front-page billing in many
newspapers. This is not just a cultural issue. Some economists maintain that the
Europeans of earlier periods brought to the United States much higher skill levels
than the Asian and Hispanic immigrants of today (Borjas 1990).

Even with changes made in the Immigration Act of 1990, most immigrants
today gain entry through the family-reunification system. This policy of giving

Figure 2. Immigrant Arrivals as a Proportion of US Population, 1850–2000

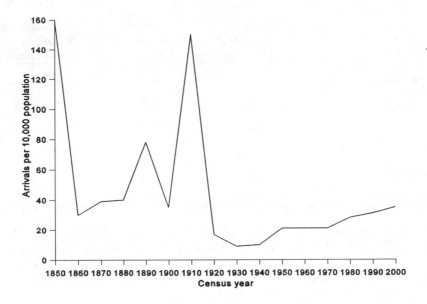

Source: US Council of Economic Advisers, 1985; data for 2000 based on projections by author.

first preference to immigrants who wish to come to the United States to reunite with family members was instituted in 1965. Today, about 80 percent of immigrants are family-sponsored, about 15 percent are political refugees, and about 5 percent are skill-based immigrants. Since enactment of the Immigration Act of 1965, the ethnic composition of immigration has changed markedly—but not in ways that most people suspect.

According to the 1981 Select Commission on Immigration, from 1800 through 1920, between 80 and 90 percent of immigrants were of European ancestry. Since then, European immigration has continually declined to comprise between 10 and 15 percent of the total immigrant flow in the mid–1980s (Moore 1989). (In very recent years, however, evidence suggests that immigration from Europe is rising sharply.) Many Americans think that the big shift in

Figure 3. Foreign-Born Population of the United States, 1850–1990

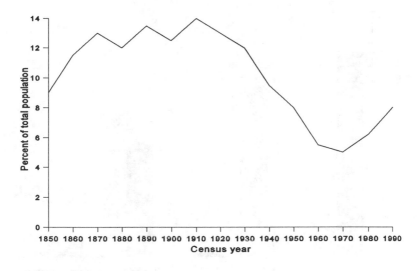

Source: US Census Bureau data.

the 1970s and 1980s was to allow entry of more Hispanics from Central America. In fact, since the 1920s immigration from the rest of North America has remained steady at between 35 and 45 percent of the total. Hispanics have been coming to the United States in large numbers for seventy years. A US General Accounting Office report (1988a) concludes that the number of immigrants from Mexico has been "quite stable in this century."

What is different today from 1965 is that European immigration has been supplanted by *Asian* immigration. Figure 4 shows that in 1965 almost half of all immigrants came from Europe and 10 percent from Asia, but that by 1990, those percentages had essentially reversed (Moore 1989). In the 1980s, the number of Asians grew by 80 percent to seven million (Dunn 1990).

The key issue then, with respect to the changing ethnic composition of America's "newest immigrants," is whether immigration from Asia has had a favorable or unfavorable impact on the US economy. This subject will be discussed in greater detail below, but for now it is worth noting that most research indicates a very high return from Cambodian, Chinese, Indian, Japanese,

Figure 4. Immigrants Admitted by Region and Period

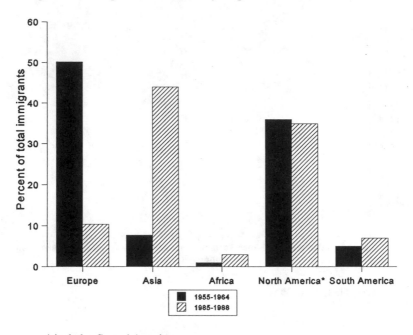

* includes Central America

Source: Statistical Yearbook of the Immigration and Naturalization Service, 1990. Washington, DC: INS, 1990, p. 39.

Pakistani, Taiwanese, and Vietnamese immigrants. The 1990 census reveals that the earnings of Asians are higher than those of any other ethnic group, including whites (Dunn 1990). The average Asian family income is $36,000, versus $29,000 for all US households.

One major reason why there has been a decline in European immigration has little to do with US immigration policy, but is because until recently, immigrants (except for a handful of refugees) from Poland, Russia, Hungary, Romania, and other former Soviet-bloc totalitarian regimes have been unable to emigrate. In the 1980s, only about 3 percent of America's immigrants came from the Eastern bloc—roughly the same number that arrived from the small island of Jamaica.

All of the above analysis shows that immigration is not at troublingly high rates today. But what about during the next century? The answer is that coming demographic changes through at least 2040 will make increased immigration more vital to the US national interest than at any time in recent history. The demographic change to which I refer is the aging of the "baby boom" generation.

In a *Wall Street Journal* editorial, Peter Francese (1990), president of American Demographics, explains the urgency of an immigration policy attuned to this impending demographic crisis:

> There are powerful demographic forces at work in the US that virtually mandate federal policy be changed to permit more immigration than we have now. The rapid increase in the number of very elderly people, combined with declining numbers of young adults and a record low population growth rate, will put this nation in a demographic vise.
>
> Paying for the income security and medical needs of the elderly while at the same time improving the educational opportunities and well-being of children will squeeze future U.S. workers in the grip of higher federal payroll taxes, state taxes and local property taxes.
> . . .
> We cannot wait 20 years to see what will happen when the baby boomers retire and ask what happened to their Social Security trust fund.
>
> The US needs to admit more immigrants now to get us out of the demographic bind.

Statistics confirm this gloomy assessment. Over the next twenty years, the number of Americans over age eighty-five and highly dependent on government programs such as Social Security and Medicare will increase from less than four million to more than six million. New entrants to the workforce (those between ages twenty and twenty-nine) will drop by about 10 percent.

A study I conducted for the California-based Alexis de Tocqueville Institute (Moore 1990b) shows that this "demographic bind" described by Francese can in part be solved through increased immigration. First, it is critical to realize that without increase immigration the "graying of the workforce," a natural consequence of the aging of the baby boom generation, will impose significant costs on future workers when the baby boomers actually retire. In 1970, there were four workers for every retired person; by 1990, there were three workers for every retired person; by 2030, there will be less than two workers for every

retiree. To provide promised health care and Social Security benefits to these
baby boomers would require nearly a 40 percent increase in payroll taxes. This
is a huge cost to impose on the next generation of workers.

Social Security Administration data (1989) suggests that because increased
immigration provides more workers immediately, the impending fiscal time
bomb can be defused by immigration. The reason for this is that every permanent
increase of 100,000 in the number of legal immigrant admissions increases
payroll receipts by roughly 0.10 percent of taxable payroll—or about $2.4 billion
each year (in 1990 dollars) (Social Security Administration 1989). If immigration levels were increased by roughly 400,000 per year, the present-value benefit
to the Social Security Trust Fund over the period 1991–2015 would be $72.2
billion. The present-value benefit to the trust fund over the next fifty years
(1991–2040) would be $292 billion (see table 2). Of course, these immigrants
will collect Social Security benefits when they retire, but they will have their
own children paying into the trust fund. Hence, increased immigration in the
next century would substantially alleviate the fiscal crisis in the Social Security
and Medicare systems without relying on raising taxes or substantially reducing
benefits.

Policy Recommendation

Historical experience shows that the United States can easily sustain an
immigration level of one million new entrants per year for the rest of this
century. In the next century, because of America's changing demographic
profile, particularly the aging of the baby boom generation, more workers
will be needed to sustain the US economy and pay the retirement costs of
current workers. This can be achieved in part by continuing to raise
immigration levels to about 1.5 million admissions per year.

America's immigration policy should encourage ethnic diversity to the
extent possible. A special immigrant visa, "freedom visas," should be established for the people of Eastern Europe, who for the past forty years have not
been permitted to immigrate to the United States. A total of 50,000 freedom
visas should be issued each year to the people of Poland, Hungary, Russia, the
Czech Republic, Slovakia, and other former Soviet-bloc countries.

3

Immigration, the Welfare State, and Taxes

The development of a modern-day welfare state in the United States and other industrialized nations has become a popular argument for substantially limiting immigration. Governor Pete Wilson of California says that his state's chronic multi-billion budget deficits are a result of social services used by low-income immigrants. Similarly, Nobel–prize winning economist Gary Becker (1992) of the University of Chicago has expressed misgivings recently about an open-door immigration policy because he fears that America's modern-day welfare system may act as a magnet to immigrants from poor countries, therefore substantially raising government outlays.

The prospect that the availability of welfare benefits would attract immigrants is a valid concern. The United States offers a substantial number of social safety-net programs to low-income Americans, most of which were not available thirty years ago. In addition to cash subsidies, such as AFDC (Aid for Families with Dependent Children, or welfare), these benefits include Food Stamps, public housing, child nutrition programs, Medicaid, unemployment insurance, and others. In some states, such as California and New York, the cash value of these benefits can exceed $14,000 a year for nonworking parents—far more than the average family income in most nations.

Are immigrants especially heavy users of the US welfare programs? Some recent studies would seem to suggest that the answer is yes. An influential and widely cited study by the Los Angeles County Board of Supervisors (1992), for example, examines the tax payments and service usage of "recent legal immigrants," "undocumented aliens," and "children of undocumented aliens" in 1991. It finds that immigrants use hundreds of millions of dollars of county services each year, including the hospital, school, and welfare systems. These immigrants make up 25 percent of all county residents, but collect 31 percent of all county services, including, dramatically, 68 percent of all county health services. Meanwhile, they pay only 10 percent of county taxes. The net result from this disproportionately high use of services, alleges the Los Angeles County Board of Supervisors, is that it cost the county $947 million in 1991 to provide government services to the immigrants, while these immigrants paid only $139 million in taxes. The immigrants also cost the school districts an estimated $1.5 billion. In short, immigrants apparently are a large drain on California's taxpayers.

It is worth describing the methodological errors of the Los Angeles County study because these same problems plague much of the research on the use of social services by immigrants. The report focuses almost exclusively on *local* services and taxes, ignoring state and federal taxes paid by immigrants. When state and federal taxes are included in the picture, the tax payments by immigrants rise to $4.3 billion per year. Since immigrants use few state services, and even fewer federal services, the surpluses supplied to federal and state coffers may very well offset the deficit to local governments. The Los Angeles County study did not address this critical question.

More important, the Los Angeles County Board of Supervisors study only examines the impact of "recent immigrants"; immigrants who arrived before 1980 are treated as US–born. But immigrants earn higher incomes, contribute more in taxes, and use less of many services the longer they have been in the United States. To exclude from a cost-benefit calculation the immigrants' impact once they have been in the United States more than ten years—that is, precisely when they start to have a high economic return—would be equivalent to assessing the cost-benefit of a child from birth until age twenty. Children would appear to be a terrible investment for the first twenty years, because they produce very little and consume very much. Like children, immigrants' short-term costs must be balanced against increasing payoffs, through higher tax payments and earnings, in the future.

When the use of public services, especially welfare, by *all immigrants* is compared with that of use of all US–born citizens, the rates are remarkably similar. A study by economist Ellen Seghal (1985) of the US Bureau of Labor Statistics examines welfare usage in 1984 of several major federal programs of immigrants who entered the United States before 1982. She finds that the share of foreign-born collecting public assistance—including unemployment compen-

Table 2. Impact of Immigrants on the Social Security Trust Fund, 1991–2065

	Increase in Social Security Revenues with 1 Million Immigrants per Year* for		
	25 Years (1991–2015)	50 Years (1991–2040)	75 Years (1991–2065)
Annual increase (percent)	0.12	0.26	0.28
Average annual increase in Trust Fund (billions)	$3.1	$6.7	$7.2
Present value in 1991 of total increase (billions)	$72.2	$292.0	$435.8

*   Assumes that the increase in net immigration is 300,000 per year (400,000 immigrating, less 100,000 emigrating).

Source: Social Security Administration, "Federal Old-Age and Survivors Insurance and Disability Insurance Trust Funds," Board of Trustees Report. Washington, DC: US Government Printing Office, April 1989; Stephen Moore, *People and American Competitiveness: Estimating the Economic Impact of Legal Immigration Reform,* Stanford, CA: Alexis de Tocqueville Institute, 1990.

sation, Food Stamps, Supplemental Security Income (SSI), and AFDC—was 12.8 percent. The percentage for US–born was 13.9 percent. She concludes that the widespread perception of immigrants as welfare abusers is wrong: "The foreign born do not seem more likely than the US–born to be recipients of government services" (p. 24).

Most research on immigrant use of welfare confirms the conclusion that immigrants are not much different in the use of social services than US–born citizens. A study by the City of New York's Office of City Planning (cited in Bogen 1986) examines the use of public assistance by a sample of the two million foreign-born in the metropolitan area in 1980. It finds that the public assistance rate was 7.7 percent for immigrants and 13.3 percent for the population as a whole.

George Borjas (1990) of the University of California examines 1970 and 1980 census data with respect to welfare (AFDC and SSI) and other economic variables. He finds that in 1970, immigrants were slightly less likely to be on welfare than native-born citizens (5.9 percent for immigrants, 6.1 percent for US–born), and that in 1980 the percentage of US–born residents on welfare was 8.0 percent, while the percentage for immigrants was 9.1 percent. This is not much of a difference. The newly released US census data for 1990 show the same result: immigrants are just slightly more dependent on welfare than US–born citizens (6 percent versus 7 percent).

Hispanic immigrants are alleged to be especially heavy users of welfare services, but the research generally does not verify this stereotype. One of the most comprehensive studies on Hispanic immigration in California was published by the Urban Institute (Muller and Espenshade 1985). The authors find that annual welfare benefits averaged $575 per California household, but less than half this amount, or $251, per Mexican immigrant household. The one public service that is used inordinately by the Mexican immigrants is education: it costs the state $1,966 for each Mexican family in public education expenditures, compared to only $872 for the average family.

A RAND Corporation analysis (McCarthy and Valdez 1985) of Mexican immigrants in California comes to much the same conclusion. The study finds that Mexican immigrants' use of schools and medical services is very high, but only because of their age profile—immigrants come when they are young. As for social services, the researchers indicate that "common perceptions that the immigrants draw heavily on welfare are not supported by either survey data or by service providers' reports." Only 5 percent of Mexicans (citizens, legal immigrants, and illegal immigrants) are found to be receiving cash assistance in 1980.

One reason immigrants do not use the welfare system excessively is that immigration involves a natural selection process of individuals who are highly motivated and energized. Immigrants come to work, not to go on welfare. The evidence supports this contention. Immigrants tend to have high labor-force participation rates and tend to work longer hours than US–born residents. Borjas (1990) found that in 1980 immigrant men were slightly more likely than US–born men to be in the labor force: 90 percent versus 89 percent (pp. 134–49). This characteristic of immigrants appears to cross ethnic groupings. For example, a study by David Hayes Bautista of the University of California at Los Angeles on the social impact of various ethnic groups in California finds that 81 percent of Latino men were in the labor force in 1990, compared to 76 percent of white men and 67 percent of black men (cited in Myer 1992, 32). Bautista concludes: "When we look at the data, we get a very different picture of Latino immigration. Rather than being viewed as a threat, it should be seen as strengthening our economy" (Myer 1992, 32).

Still, for many financially strapped cities the issue of funding services to immigrants is of growing concern. The problem for localities is that at least half of the government services used by immigrants are provided by localities, but according to the RAND Corporation, an estimated two-thirds of the tax payments by immigrants are paid to the federal government, primarily in the form of income and Social Security taxes, and less than 15 percent are paid to local governments (McCarthy and Valdez 1985). The Urban Institute study on immigration in California in the 1970s thoroughly documents this financing mismatch problem (Muller and Espenshade 1985). It finds that in 1980 the fiscal deficit at the state level was $1,779 per Mexican household, and Los Angeles County lost $466 per immigrant household. But the federal government enjoyed a healthy fiscal windfall from each Mexican household in Los Angeles County. It is important to note that the Urban Institute researchers find that even though the value of the local services California immigrants use is greater than the amount they pay in local taxes, they are still a significant economic asset to the California communities in which they reside. Muller and Espenshade (1985) conclude: "The over-all economic benefits accruing to the average Los Angeles household from the presence of Mexican immigrants probably outweigh the economic costs of fiscal deficits."

Researchers have begun to examine the issue of whether the total taxes paid by the immigrants at all levels of government cover the total costs of public services they use at all levels of government. The most comprehensive study on this topic was conducted by economist Julian Simon (1984) at the University of Maryland. Simon uses Census Bureau data from 1975 to calculate the total cost of public services used by immigrants at various lengths of stay in the United States to build a lifetime benefit profile for immigrants. He assumes, for instance, that immigrants who entered in 1972 are typical of immigrants after three years in the United States, immigrants who entered in 1971 were typical of immigrants after four years, and so on. The services examined include health care, Social Security, unemployment insurance, education, welfare, and an allowance for other government programs such as infrastructure. Simon then uses the same procedure to build a lifetime profile of taxes paid by immigrants. He does this by examining the earnings of immigrants over their working years and deducing their tax payments, which are assumed to be roughly proportional to income.

Simon finds that in their early years in the United States, immigrants use less public services than US–born citizens, but that in their later years, they begin to use roughly the same amount of services. This is partly because newly arriving immigrants collect almost no benefits from the largest public assistance program, Social Security, and because newly arriving immigrants are not eligible for many welfare programs, such as unemployment insurance. For example, for their first fifteen years in the United States, immigrants use roughly $1,500 of services (in 1975 dollars) each year, whereas after fifteen years, immigrants use almost $2,300 of services. The average for US–born citizens was also about $2,300. As for earnings and taxes, for the first five to ten years, immigrant earnings are below those of US–born workers; after ten to fifteen years, the earnings match those of natives; and after fifteen years, the immigrants' earnings rise permanently above US–born earnings. Several independent studies, including Chiswick (1978) verify this lifetime earning pattern.

Simon then creates an immigrant balance sheet by placing the taxes paid and public services used side by side to assess the value of immigrant as one would a physical investment:

> In every year following entry (until the immigrants themselves retire, at which time their children are supporting them through the Social Security and Medicare system) immigrants benefit natives through the public coffers. And a calculation of the net present value of the stream of difference shows that immigrants are a remarkably good investment at any conceivable rate of discount.
>
> At a 3 percent rate of discount (the riskless rate of real return on a government security), the lifetime benefit of immigrants to US citizens via the tax code is roughly $20,000. "One may conclude," states Simon, "that the average immigrant is an excellent investment on almost any reasonable set of parameter estimates" (Simon 1984).

In sum, legal immigrants do pay their own way. This conclusion raises a critical government financing issue: If immigrants contribute positively to the overall fiscal balance of federal coffers, but are a fiscal drain on the local level, steps could be taken to reduce the disparity and at the same time leave all levels of government with a more improved fiscal position than if the immigrants did not come at all. One potential solution would be for the federal government to reimburse local governments for a portion of the costs of providing services to immigrants.

Finally, we need to make a special examination of the fiscal impact of refugees. Refugees have some very different characteristics than economic immigrants. Refugees generally use substantially more services than immigrants; they are more likely to be unemployed or outside the workforce; and they have much lower earnings than immigrants. One of the most comprehensive studies to date of refugees' economic performance is by Susan Forbes (1985) of the Refugee Policy Group. Forbes reviews most of the research on refugees and uncovers several troubling findings for the newest arrivals. In 1984, 64 percent of the US population was in the labor force, but only 55 percent of refugees were. Seven percent of Americans were unemployed, compared to 15 percent of refugees.

Unlike economic immigrants, who are ineligible for many public assistance programs, newly arriving refugees are immediately eligible for special resettlement and adjustment assistance (a package that can be worth up to $5,000), in addition to all normal public assistance benefits—and large numbers take advantage of this eligibility. During the first year of admission, about 75 percent of refugees are on public assistance; after their second year in the United States, more than half are on public assistance; and even after their third year, roughly a third collect some form of cash assistance from the government (Forbes 1985).

The good news is, however, that refugees do climb the ladder of economic progress in much the same manner, albeit at a slower rate, as immigrants (see Moore 1990a). For example, according to the Office of Refugee Resettlement (1989), half of the Southeast Asian refugees who arrived in the United States in 1985, half were unemployed at the end of 1985, but only 20 percent were unemployed in 1986, 9 percent in 1987, and 5 percent in 1988. That is, after four years, the 1985 refugees' unemployment rate matched the national rate. Labor-force participation also rises steadily over time for males. Rita J. Simon and Julian L. Simon (1984) find that in 1981, 42 percent of Soviet Jewish male refugees worked at least thirty-five hours a week, whereas 91 percent who had arrived before 1973 did. Finally, Barry Chiswick (1978) finds that, as with immigrants, refugees' incomes rise steadily over time, but that it takes much longer for refugees to "catch up" to the national average than for legal immigrants.

Still, the very high rates of dependency among refugees during their first three years in the United States is disturbing. Immediate access to welfare is a policy that is bad for refugees and US taxpayers. There is substantial evidence that the availability of welfare deters and delays the entry of refugees into the labor force. In California, the state with the highest welfare benefits, 85 percent of refugees who had been in the United States three years or less in 1984 were on public assistance; in Texas, where welfare benefits are less than half the level in California, less than 20 percent of similar refugees were on welfare (Forbes 1985). The availability of generous welfare benefits "appears to sap refugees' economic energies," conclude economists Reginald Baker and David North (1984) in their study of the 1975 Southeast Asian refugees. US welfare policies designed to provide a compassionate safety-net for refugees, may be doing the newcomers more harm than good (Moore 1990a).

On balance, however, immigrants and refugees appear to be a good deal for the United States: their taxes cover the costs of their public services. So concludes the 1985 *Economic Report of the President,* which includes an exhaustive investigation into the economic effects of immigrants. Its findings on the fiscal impact of immigrants summarizes well the fiscal impact of immigrants:

> On the whole, international migrants appear to pay their own way from a public finance standpoint. Most come to the United States to work, and government benefits do not appear to be a major attraction. Some immigrants arrive with fairly high educational levels, and their training imposes no substantial costs on the public. Their rising levels of income produce a rising stream of tax payments to all levels of government. Their initial dependence on welfare benefits is usually limited, and they finance their participation in Social Security retirement benefits with years of contributions. (Council of Economic Advisers 1986)

Policy Recommendation

Immigrants as a group do not abuse the welfare system. Some do, however. One of the long-standing conditions of entry for immigrants is that they not become a public charge. This policy should be more strictly enforced. For their first five years in the United States, immigrants should be ineligible for most cash and non-cash welfare benefits, with emergency medical care being a notable exception. Immigrants who go on welfare during their first five years in the United States should be denied continued residency.

The explicit purpose of refugee assistance programs is to "help refugees achieve economic self-sufficiency within the shortest time possible following their arrival in the United States." In practice, these programs have had precisely the opposite effect, contributing to a culture of dependency within refugee communities. Most special refugee assistance programs should be eliminated. Refugee assistance should be privately provided by nonprofit resettlement agencies and ethnic associations.

4

Immigrants, Jobs, and Wages

> In Kemah, Texas, the commercial fishermen who had long worked
> the Gulf Coast found their waters dotted with Vietnamese in rival
> boats. The Vietnamese were here legally, admitted as refugees. They
> had scrimped to lease or buy their fishing craft. The working class
> whites had initially tolerated them. When the Vietnamese took
> low-income jobs cleaning fish or working in restaurant kitchens, they
> were acceptable. But when they became fishermen—and competi-
> tors—attitudes toward them changed. The unpleasant fact is that the
> Vietnamese work harder and longer and under more difficult condi-
> tions than do most Americans. (Fallows 1983, 61)

Do immigrants compete with American workers for jobs? Today, nearly
twenty years after Vietnamese refugees first arrived in towns such as
Kemah, Texas, along the Gulf Coast, the fishing industry is dominated by these
resourceful and hard-working immigrants. US–born fishermen have unquestionably been displaced. Such displacement occurs regularly in a market-based
economy. New product lines displace the old; new technological innovations
displace standard procedures and sometimes entire industries; efficient workers
displace the inefficient. There are almost always economic losers under such
competitions, even though the society as a whole is almost always left wealthier
and better off. Indeed, the pressure of competition is one of the engines of
economic growth under a capitalist economy. In this case, American fishermen
were simply out-worked by refugees who came from across the globe.

The fear that immigrants will diminish job opportunities for American-born workers has been the single most persistent argument against a liberal US immigration policy for at least the past hundred years. A typical claim is that for every hundred new immigrants, sixty-five American workers lose their jobs (Huddle 1982). Politicians opposed to more immigration ask, Why do we need more immigrants when we already have millions unemployed? Union leaders tend to be particularly concerned about immigration and job competition. For example, the American Engineering Association (1990), a lobbying group representing US–born engineers, charges that immigrant engineers "work at vastly reduced wages and often replace the citizen on the job."

At first stroke, it seems intuitive that immigrants must harm US workers. It makes sense that immigrants could be substitutes for American workers in similar occupations and that the immigrants' arrival would lead to higher unemployment for such workers. Economic theory would suggest that in competitive labor markets, the longer-run labor market impact of immigrant workers is felt not through higher unemployment, but rather through an adjustment *downward* in wage levels to accommodate the new arrivals. Even this would be unwelcome news to current US workers and would validate their concerns about immigration.

On the other hand, there are countervailing economic forces at work that lead to expansion of the economy and the creation of jobs in response to new immigrants.[1] Immigrants may create jobs in at least the following six ways:

1) Immigrants expand the demand for goods and services through their own consumption.

2) Immigrants may contribute to total output and productivity in a country through the savings they bring with them.

3) Immigrants are highly entrepreneurial and create jobs through the businesses they start.

4) Immigrants may fill vital niches in the low- and high-skilled ends of the labor market, thus creating subsidiary jobs for US workers.

5) Immigrants, particularly low-paid immigrants, may save declining industries or US industries under intense competition from imports.

6) Immigrants may contribute to economies of scale in production and the growth of markets.

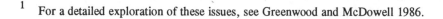

[1] For a detailed exploration of these issues, see Greenwood and McDowell 1986.

Economic theory alone cannot offer a definitive answer to the issue of whether immigrants harm US workers. Fortunately, there is a wealth of empirical evidence on the labor market impact of immigrants—most of it completed within the past ten years—that does provide answers.

Immigration and Unemployment

A recent study by Richard Vedder, Lowell Galloway, and myself (1990) is a useful place to start this discussion because the study is a time-series analysis of the relationship between immigration and unemployment over the past century (1890–1989). The study attempts to explain year-to-year fluctuations in the national unemployment rate using four measures: 1) immigration, defined as the percentage of the American population that is foreign-born in each year; 2) wages; 3) prices (the consumer price index); and 4) productivity, or output per hour worked. The model explains 75 percent of the variation in unemployment over this hundred–year period.

If higher levels of immigration cause an aggregate increase in unemployment on the national level, then we would expect that the higher the percentage of foreign-born at any one time, the higher the subsequent unemployment rate (if other variables are held constant). Our results, however, show a statistically significant *negative* relationship between immigration to the United States and subsequent national unemployment.

One might argue that low unemployment causes high immigration rather than the other way around. This is the idea that US economic conditions act as a "pull factor" for immigration. And, indeed, in the nineteenth century and the early part of the twentieth century there is strong evidence that this pull factor determined the annual size of the immigration stream (Easterlin 1968). However, by 1925, America's open-door policy had ended, and since 1953, the annual legal immigration level has bumped against the congressionally imposed predetermined ceiling every year. This has erased the influence of the pull factor in determining the size of immigration from year to year, because there are always more immigrants who wish to come than are permitted to come—regardless of whether unemployment is high or low in any given year. Meanwhile, the push factor—the economic conditions of the immigrant's home country—has become the major factor in determining the composition of the immigrant flow from year to year. When we examine the data series starting in 1925 and then again in 1953, we obtain the same general results, although the negative relationship is not as strong. And so the evidence suggests that, on a nationwide basis, higher levels of immigration are associated with subsequent lower rates of unemployment—precisely the opposite of what immigrant opponents argue.

In our 1990 study, we also disaggregate immigration and unemployment down to the state level. We examine the relationship between the foreign-born populations of each of the forty-eight contiguous states in 1980 (as well as four other labor market factors) and the unemployment rates in these states for four years—1982, 1983, 1984, and 1985. This model predicts 83 percent of the variance in state unemployment (Vedder, Galloway, and Moore 1990).

This model causes us not only to reject the hypothesis that immigration causes unemployment, but to confirm a statistically significant *negative* relationship between a state's percentage of foreign-born in 1980 and its unemployment rate in subsequent years. The results make sense if we consider on an observational level the states where unemployment has been high and where it has been low. In the 1980s, California, Florida, Massachusetts, and Texas, for instance, had very high immigration rates, but lower than average unemployment rates. States such as Iowa, West Virginia, and Wyoming had virtually no immigration, but high and rising unemployment.

Roughly three-fourths of all immigrants reside in large cities. The economic conditions in cities such as Los Angeles, Miami, New York, and San Diego are hugely influenced by immigrants (the following section discusses this local economic impact in greater detail). The labor market impact of immigration may not be detectable in national or even state unemployment figures, but immigrants may have a significant negative impact in the local labor markets where they reside.

A study by economists Julian Simon, myself, and Richard Sullivan (1993) explores the issue of whether immigrants add to the unemployment rate in major cities. The study examines how the immigration rate (new immigrant arrivals to a city as a percentage of the population of the city) affects the change in the unemployment rate in seventy-seven major immigrant-receiving cities between 1960 and 1977. Using a pooled regression technique (which combines the cross-section and time-series data), we examine the impact of immigration on the local unemployment rates for various lag periods between one and five years. For example, we explored what happens to the unemployment rate in a city in 1973, 1974, 1975, and 1976, in response to immigration into the city in 1972.

We find a very small, but statistically insignificant, positive relationship between immigration to a city and unemployment two years later. We find that an upper-bound estimate of the amount of unemployment created by an immigrant's arrival in a local labor market is the one-time loss of 0.85

person-years of employment for a US worker over the immigrant's working life. This is roughly the equivalent of saying that every thirty immigrant arrivals leads to one US worker becoming permanently unemployed. This is a very tiny effect that is far from the typical rhetoric of a hundred immigrants displacing sixty-five workers.

Other research examining immigration and unemployment in local labor markets comes to similar conclusions. Economists Michael Greenwood and G. L. Hunt (1984) examine the employment effects of immigrants in a sample of fifty-seven metropolitan areas between 1958 and 1975. They find that each employed "in-migrant" leads to 1.26 jobs (the job for the immigrant plus 0.26 additional jobs); conversely, each "out-migrant" leads to the loss of 0.26 jobs over time. The researchers find a net displacement effect in only three of the fifty-seven cities: Baltimore; Grand Rapids, Michigan; and Los Angeles. In sum, Greenwood and Hunt's analysis can be interpreted to mean not only that the job market stretches to accommodate an influx of immigrants, but also that employment expands to create additional job opportunities for the US–born workers in the area.

Special concerns have been raised of late about the impact of immigrants on minorities, particularly on urban blacks. Here again, the research suggests that these concerns are overstated. As part of their comprehensive study on immigration in California in the 1970s, Muller and Espenshade (1985) examined the job competition between immigrants and blacks in 247 metropolitan areas in 1980. They not only reject the notion that Hispanic or Mexican immigrants reduce job prospects for blacks, but they also conclude that immigrants and blacks are "complements in production." In other words, the presence of immigrants may promote the upward job mobility of black workers.

Many additional studies have examined the economic impact of immigration in specific high-immigrant cities, including Houston, Miami, Los Angeles, and New York. This issue is treated separately in the following section, but the general thrust of the findings confirms that immigrants have a positive effect on the labor market.

Immigration and Unemployment in Specific Industries

Immigrants not only are concentrated in specific metropolitan areas, they also are employed disproportionately in specific industries. Their entry into these sectoral labor markets may cause significant displacement of US workers that hold jobs in those industries, just as the Vietnamese displaced the Texas fishermen.

Economists Joseph Altonji and David Card (1990) of Princeton University examine the labor market changes in ten high-immigrant worker industries, including apparel, leather, agriculture, furniture, light manufacturing, and household services. Immigrants constitute anywhere from 15 to 40 percent of all workers in these industries. Moreover, for the period examined, 1970–80, the percentage of immigrant workers in these industries expanded by an average of 10 percent. Therefore, one would expect that if immigrants displace US–born workers at all, it would be observable in these fields. What Altonji and Card find is that indeed there was some displacement of US workers, especially in industries such as apparel, where the immigrant share of employment rose sharply during the period in question. However, when they examine unemployment, earnings, and labor-force participation of US workers in the cities where the immigrants work, they find that "there was no consistent pattern of adverse effects on any native group, for any indicator of labor market success." Displaced workers evidently had no trouble finding jobs in other industries in these cities. Altonji and Card also find some evidence that "industries which employ low-skill workers operating in high-immigrant markets have outperformed others in terms of employment growth." Therefore, they conclude that the labor market impact on US workers of increased immigration in the 1970s "was minor."

In some industries immigrants have undeniably taken jobs from US–born workers. An example is the contract cleaning industry. Mines and Avina (1985) find a dramatic increase in legal and illegal immigrants in the contract cleaning workforce in the early 1980s in California. This industry, especially in downtown areas such as Los Angeles, was heavily dominated by large, unionized firms in the 1970s. The small immigrant-worker firms handled only small buildings. But Mines and Avina find that by 1983, when wages and benefits in the unionized firms averaged nearly $13 per hour, the immigrant-labor firms had begun to carve into the unionized market by offering lower prices, and that by 1985, the unionized firms had been forced to hire lower-cost immigrant workers as well. Mines and Avina find that the number of black janitors in Los Angeles dropped by more than 75 percent between 1977 and 1985, and that for the unionized American-born workers remaining in the industry, the average wage and benefit package had fallen to between $5.75 and $6.40 per hour. Mines and Avina conclude that the switch to immigrant workers (legal and illegal) in the janitorial services industry "clearly displaced native workers." Moreover, wages fell and work hours increased.

Another California industry that has been impacted by immigrants is restaurant services. Kitchen work in many California towns is predominated by legal and illegal immigrants. In San Diego, the US General Accounting Office (1988b) estimates that three-fourths of all kitchen work is done by illegal immigrants. The argument is made that eliminating illegal immigrants from these jobs would force restaurant owners to pay higher wages to attract low-skilled American workers. Yet, according to an analysis by the US Department of Labor (1989), "a complete restructuring of the restaurant industry would eliminate many of the best jobs in full service establishments if these [immigrant] workers were unavailable, and hence it is difficult to conclude that native workers would benefit."

This appears to be the case in many of the low-skilled industries that are predominantly served by immigrant workers. In 1989 the US Congress requested that, as part of the President's Comprehensive Triennial Report on Immigration, the US Department of Labor examine the impact of immigrants on job opportunities for US workers. The US Department of Labor report (1989) contends that "some substitution/displacement occurs in some low-skilled occupations." But, notably, in assessing the general employment impact of immigrants, the researchers find that even where this displacement occurs, "the fact that such effects are invisible at higher levels of aggregation suggests that those directly or indirectly displaced are absorbed elsewhere in the labor market."

The growing body of literature on immigration and unemployment rates exhibits a remarkable degree of consensus in concluding that either there is no displacement effect or that the displacement that is evident is virtually insignificant. The Labor Department report (1989), which reviews research findings from over a hundred studies on the impact of immigration on unemployment and is probably the most exhaustive study on the subject ever conducted, concludes:

> Neither US workers nor most minority workers appear to be adversely affected by immigration—especially during periods of economic expansion . . . The preponderance of the evidence suggests that immigrant workers, by filling low paid and low-skilled jobs, complement the activities of many higher-skilled native-born workers and thereby protect many better paying US jobs. However, these complementary gains may be achieved at the cost of certain losses for the less skilled.

One year later, economist George Borjas (1990) of the University of California Santa Barbara corroborated this conclusion. He writes:

> The methodological arsenal of modern econometrics cannot detect a single shred of evidence that immigrants have a sizeable adverse impact on the earnings and employment opportunities of natives in the US . . . Although the conjecture that immigrants take jobs away from natives has been a prime force behind efforts to make immigration policy more restrictive throughout American history, there is no empirical evidence that the displacement effect is important (at least in recent years).

How Immigrants Create Jobs

Above I suggested that immigrants may create more jobs than they take, identifying several ways that immigrants contribute to additional employment. One of these ways is through their purchasing power. When immigrants come to the United States, they immediately raise the demand for US goods and services (Greenwood and McDowell 1986). They shop for food in US grocery stores; they move into apartments or homes, stimulating more demand for housing construction; they eat at American restaurants; and so on. All of these activities lead to more jobs for US workers. In other words, as producers, immigrants fill jobs, but as consumers they create jobs.

Another way that immigrants increase jobs, alluded to above, is by helping to save industries that may not otherwise survive in the United States. The fruit and vegetable industry in California is an example of an industry that may be incapable of competing with its counterpart in Mexico were it not for a steady supply of low-paid immigrants. Another example is the garment industry, which has been dominated by new immigrants for more than a hundred years:

From its inception, the US garment industry has been inextricably linked to immigration. With the advent of a ready to wear clothing industry in the 1880s, Irish, Swedish and German dressmakers were succeeded by Italians and Eastern Europeans. By 1900 the industry was already ethnically differentiated. Men's clothing was produced by Italian women working out of the home; other apparel came from factories owned and operated by Europeans most of whom were Jewish. As European immigration slowed in the 1930s, other groups, especially native-born black women from the south and Puerto Ricans took over production roles. The latest groups of women to succeed them in the industry are Chinese, Korean, Dominican and Mexican immigrants. (US Department of Labor 1989, 109)

By the late 1980s, for example, there were some 600 garment factories in the Chinatown section of lower Manhattan, with employee payrolls of more than $200 million (Kotkin 1992, 111; Wong 1988, 173–75). In this industry, at least, the continued entry of immigrants has actually boosted employment for US packagers, wholesale workers, truckers, and middle-level managers. Among those familiar with the industry, few doubt that without immigrant workers, the US apparel industry would have moved entirely overseas to Korea, Hong Kong, and Singapore. Richard Rothstein, former manager of the Amalgamated Clothing and Textile Workers Union, concedes, "Prohibiting employment of immigrants in this industry, the only workers willing to labor in minimum and near-minimum garment jobs, would only accelerate the destruction of the domestic industry" (quoted in Kotkin 1989, 24). Many other sectors of the economy, including the shoe, furniture, poultry, and food-processing industries are similarly dependent upon the replenishment of immigrant labor for their survival.

Foreign-born workers have been lifeblood for several declining manufacturing industries that face intense competition from low-priced imports. Muller and Espenshade (1985) conclude that one of the positive side-effects of immigrants in Los Angeles was in increasing the profitability of US manufacturers located there. They estimate that if it were not for Mexican immigration, 53,000 production jobs and 12,000 management jobs would have disappeared in the manufacturing sector. This loss of jobs would have had a further contractionary effect on the overall Los Angeles economy, causing 25,000 more incidental jobs to be lost. The point to emphasize is that even lower-skilled immigrant workers create job opportunities for US workers in hidden but often significant ways.

Table 3. Self-Employment among Immigrants in the United States and Canada

	Self-Employed Workers (percent)	Annual Income of Self-Employed Workers (native dollars)
All US-born workers	7.1	n.a.
Immigrant US workers	9.2	n.a.
All US Men	11.4	23,000
Immigrant US men	12.2	24,000
All Canadian-born workers	6.8	15,000
Immigrant Canadian workers	7.9	16,000

Note: US figures are for 1980; Canadian figures are for 1981.

Sources: George J. Borjas, *Friends or Strangers: The Impact of Immigration on the U.S. Economy.* New York: Basic Books, 1990; Iven Light and Angel A. Sanchez, "Immigrant Entrepreneurs in 272 SMSAs,"*Sociological Perspectives* (October 1987): 373–99; and Elliot L. Tepper, "Self-Employment in Canada among Immigrants of Different Ethno-Cultural Backgrounds," *Employment and Immigration in Canada* (November 1988).

Of course, it is not just low-skilled immigrants who assist US industries. At the opposite end of the spectrum, highly trained and educated immigrants have created new high-technology industries that are now flourishing in the United States and have created hundreds of thousands of subsidiary jobs for US workers. (This phenomenon is sufficiently important to the American economy that I dedicate an entire section below to a discussion of it.)

Immigrants are highly entrepreneurial. Their propensity to start new businesses generates new jobs in the US economy. Table 3, which compares the rate of self-employment for immigrants with that of native-born workers in the United States and Canada, shows that immigrants are about 10 to 20 percent more likely to start a new business than native-born workers. Moreover, the incomes of the immigrant entrepreneurs tend to be slightly higher than those of the native-born entrepreneurs, which suggests that immigrant businesses may be more successful on average (Borjas 1990, 164–67). Examining the business-creation process in 247 metropolitan areas in the 1970s, Light and Sanchez (1987) conclude that up to half of all new businesses started were immigrant-owned.

It would be tempting to conclude that because immigrant businesses tend to be small, family-based, and concentrated in ethnic neighborhoods, they are therefore an insignificant source of new jobs in the US economy. This is far from being the case. The US Department of Labor study (1989) of immigrant-owned businesses concludes that "their vitality means that they are prodigious creators of jobs and contribute substantially to an area's overall economic vitality" (p. 198). It notes that the severe decline in business establishments and employment in retail trade in New York City in the 1970s was reversed in the 1980s, in large part through "heavy immigrant entrepreneurship" (p. 198).

Immigrants and Wages

It is quite possible that the primary impact of immigrant workers is on wage rates rather than on unemployment rates. This would be consistent with economic theory, at least as a short-run effect. For example, if 100 new immigrant construction workers enter a town with 500 US–born construction workers, construction firms may accommodate these new arrivals by expanding the number of construction jobs available, and also by lowering wages and benefits for all construction workers. The US–born construction workers would not lose their jobs, but they would suffer a decline in income.

Is this theoretical impact of immigration observed in US labor markets? Economist Jeffrey Williamson (1982) studies immigration and wage rates before 1925 and concludes that immigration had a negative impact on local wages: "Surely, in the absence of mass migrations, the real wage rate would have risen faster and inequality trends would have been less pronounced."

This assessment appears to be overly pessimistic, however. Even with very heavy immigration rates—much larger than current rates—the real wage rate rose substantially and almost uninterruptedly from 1800 to 1925, and it rose at a much faster pace than it has in recent decades. This is because immigrants had positive impacts that offset the negative effects to drive wages upward in the nineteenth century. These offsetting effects included contributions of immigrants to the process of capital accumulation, technical progress, and economies of scale. We can only speculate as to whether lower immigration in earlier periods would have caused wages to rise faster than they did, but the important lesson is that heavy immigration is not incompatible with steadily rising wage rates.

Many studies have investigated immigration and wage rates in recent decades, and on balance, the evidence suggests that immigration has a very small negative impact on wages in the short term, and that even this impact is eliminated over time. Economists Gregory Defreitas and Adriana Marshall (1984) look at the impact of foreign-born manufacturing workers on manufacturing wages in thirty-five major metropolitan areas from 1970 to 1978. They find that after controlling for the metropolitan unemployment rate, the change in the cost of living, and unionization, "the wage-dampening effect of foreign labor only becomes significant once immigrant concentrations in manufacturing reach a threshold of 20 percent of the workforce." Other studies that examine wages in particular industries, such as apparel, find similar small negative wage effects (see US Department of Labor, 1990, 97–150; Butcher and Card 1991).

When immigration rates are related to overall wage changes in an area, the impact is nearly nonexistent. For example, Defreitas (1988) studies the impact of Hispanic immigration on low-skilled urban wage rates from 1975 to 1985 and finds that wage rates of low-skilled American workers who should be competitors with Hispanic workers, on balance, were unaffected. Only wages of black females were negatively impacted and that impact was very small.

Most research finds that the only group whose wages are negatively affected by immigration are earlier immigrant arrivals. Robert Topel (1990) of the University of Chicago examines wage rates between 1970 and 1980 in 122 metropolitan areas and finds:

> Increased immigration has a modest adverse impact on the wages of the immigrants themselves and on the wages of earlier waves of immigrants, but has little if any impact on the wages of the young black and Hispanic Americans who are likely to be the next closest substitutes. Neither the employment nor the wages of less educated black and white natives worsened noticeably in cities where immigrant shares of the population rose in the 1970s.

This seems to be a standard conclusion in the existing research. Borjas (1990) summarizes the findings of seven major studies of the relationship between immigration and US wage rates, as shown in table 4. He maintains that this evidence suggests that "native and immigrant workers are, on average, weak substitutes in production" (Borjas 1990, 86–90). Of particular importance are

Table 4. The Impact of Immigrants on Native Earnings

	Change in native wages resulting from a 10 percent increase in the number of immigrants (percent)
All native-born Americans	-0.2
White Men	-0.2 to -0.1
Black Men	-0.3 to +0.2
Women	+0.2 to +0.5
Young Blacks	-0.1
Young Hispanics	-0.3 to +0.2
Manufacturing Workers	-0.4

Source: Reprinted by permission from George J. Borjas, *Friends or Strangers: The Impact of Immigration on the US Economy.* New York: Basic Books, 1990.

his findings that 1) immigrants actually may slightly *raise* the wages of black workers; 2) illegal immigration has virtually no impact whatsoever on US wage rates, contrary to popular mythology; and 3) the main negative impact is on immigrants themselves. "Recent econometric research," he concludes, "has not been able to establish a single instance in which the increase in the supply of immigrants had a significant adverse impact on the earnings of natives."

Research recently has become available on the impact of the heavy immigration in the 1980s on wage rates of US workers. Butcher and Card (1991) examine Current Population Survey data on wage rates in twenty-four high-immigrant cities from 1979 to 1989. They confirm Borjas's conclusion that wage rates were not reduced by immigration: "Our empirical analysis reveals large differences across cities in the relative growth rates of wages and low and high-priced workers. Nevertheless, these differences bear little or no relation to the size of immigrant inflows." In fact, Butcher and Card not only conclude that wages on the low end of the labor market were unaffected by immigration, they also find that "higher immigration is associated with more rapid increases" at the high end of the wage scale in these cities.

The presence of illegal immigrants in the US labor market often is said to be especially harmful to US workers. In fact, the 1986 Immigration Reform and Control Act was designed to keep undocumented aliens out of the job market by imposing sanctions on US employers found to have hired illegals. However, one of the most comprehensive studies on illegals in the labor market, by Bean, Lewis, and Taylor (1988) finds that their impact is mostly beneficial: based on 1980 Census Bureau estimates for illegal Mexican immigration in forty-seven metropolitan areas, they find no evidence of an adverse wage impact. In fact, they conclude that "the effects of undocumented Mexican immigration on the earnings of other groups may be small and in some cases may be positive." They believe that illegal immigrants are probably complements to US citizens on the job.

In sum, there is little or no scientific support for the common complaint that admitting immigrants into the United States hurts American workers. There is also no evidence to support the hypothesis that if immigrants were not allowed to enter the country, working conditions and wages for low-skilled American workers would be elevated. It is important to emphasize that these studies examine the short-term labor market impact of immigrants. Over the long term, real wages are determined almost exclusively by productivity changes—and, by raising US productivity levels and output over time, immigrants undoubtedly have contributed to rising real wages and more generous compensation for American workers.

Policy Recommendation

There is no basis for restricting immigration to protect the wages and employment opportunities of US workers. In addition, because immigrants can fill vital niches in the labor market, the process for allowing US businesses to recruit foreign-born workers with exceptional talents or to fill positions in labor-shortage occupations should be streamlined and largely deregulated. Under current law, employers who wish to bring an immigrant worker to the United States must receive certification from the US Department of Labor and prove that there are no qualified US workers available for the job at the prevailing wage rate. The employer also must document that the immigrant recruitment will not harm the wages or working conditions of US workers. This process often leads to delays of three years or more for US companies to bring high-skilled workers to the United States (Kittredge 1989). Employer-sponsored immigration makes US industries more competitive in global markets and does not threaten US workers.

5

Are the New Immigrants Worse than the Old?

> The [new immigrants] have remained strangers in the land, residing apart by themselves, and adhering to the customs and usages of their own country. It seems impossible for them to assimilate with our own people or to make any change in their habits or modes of living. As they have grown in number the people [of California] see, or believe they see, in the facility of immigration . . . great danger that at no distant day the state will be overrun by them unless prompt action is taken to restrict their immigration. (Chae Chan Ping v. US, 130 US 581 [1889], 595)

This may sound like a modern-day diatribe over the social and economic impact of America's new immigrants from Central America and Asia, but it is not. This passage was written a hundred years ago by justices of the US Supreme Court when they upheld the constitutionality of the Chinese Exclusion laws of the 1880s. At the time, Americans were fearful of "yellow hordes" of immigrants coming to the United States and undermining workers' wages while radically changing the white European culture.[2]

---

[2] For a fascinating and comprehensive analysis of American xenophobia at the turn of the century, see Higham 1963.

Opposition to immigration in the United States is not new; it has been a pervasive attitude among Americans at least since the nation gained its independence (R. Simon 1984a). Nor is it uncommon for our political leaders to express worrisome reservations about the quality of immigrants coming to America. Ben Franklin spurned the German immigrants of the eighteenth century as "generally the most stupid of their own nation," adding: "It is almost impossible to remove any prejudices they entertain" (cited in R. Simon 1984a). Calvin Coolidge spoke of preserving an "America for Americans." For a country that has a romantic vision of itself as "a nation of immigrants," Americans have almost always been hostile to immigration (R. Simon 1984a).

Surveys of American public opinion regarding immigration over the past century reveal a fascinating consistency in attitudes and prejudices. For example, since at least as far back as the turn of the century, Americans have believed that previous immigrants were valuable and honorable citizens, but that the current wave was much worse than those who came before (R. Simon 1984a). Hence, in the late 1800s, the immigrants from Ireland were regarded as the dregs of Europe and constantly confronted "Irish Need Not Apply" signs. The large immigrant flows from Italy were derided as "dagos," and "no better than the Negroes." National xenophobia directed toward the Chinese and Japanese led to the exclusionary laws of the late nineteenth century. In the 1930s, opposition to the "rising tide" of European Jews reached such a feverish pitch that tens of thousands were barred entry, many of whom tragically perished in the Holocaust. More recently, Cubans who fled Castro in the 1950s and 1960s and Vietnamese and Cambodians who fled communism in the 1970s and 1980s have been singled out as unassimilable.

In sum, virtually every group of immigrants that has come to America has been denounced at the time of their entry as the undesirables of Europe, Asia, Central America—or wherever they came from. We now know that virtually every one of these groups has made immense contributions to US society, and eventually—albeit in many cases reluctantly—has mixed into the great American melting pot. In short, for over a century, those who have questioned the benefits of the "new immigrants" have a perfect track record of being unfailingly wrong.

It should therefore come as no great surprise that the most consistent, and seemingly the most persuasive, complaint about immigration today is that the groups that are coming now lack the skills, education, drive, language skills, and inclination to assimilate that characterized previous immigrant waves. In short, the argument is made that although immigrants have been good and virtuous in the past, they are now of questionable quality.

This argument cannot be immediately dismissed. Some of America's most prominent immigration scholars have uncovered evidence of declining quality among America's "new immigrants." Principal among these researchers is economist George Borjas (1990), who declares:

> The skill composition of the immigrant flow entering the United States has deteriorated significantly in the past two or three decades; this decay in immigration skills justifies a reassessment of the economic benefits and costs of immigration.

Borjas supplies some compelling evidence to substantiate these claims. Using census data he shows that from 1940 through 1980, the level of schooling, number of hours worked, labor-force participation rates, and earnings of immigrants have steadily declined relative to US workers, while immigrants' unemployment rates have steadily risen. For example, Borjas reveals that in 1940, immigrants' wages were 13 percent above those of US workers; in 1950, their wages were equal to that of US workers; in 1960, their wages had fallen to 8 percent below US workers; by 1970, they had fallen to 10 percent below; and by 1980, to fully 17 percent below US workers (pp. 48–52). This means that the average immigrant earns $5,000 per year less than the average immigrant in 1960. According to Borjas's calculations, if immigrant skills had not fallen, total income in the United States in 1980 would have been $8. 5 billion higher.

There are a number of reasons not to be too disturbed by Borjas's findings, however. First, the decline in skills and education that has been reported is relative to the skills and education of US–born workers. For example, there has been an improvement in immigrant quality over time, but this improvement simply has not kept pace with the improvements in education and skills of US–born workers. Sociologists Portes and Rumbaut (1990) compare the education levels of recent immigrants (entering between 1975 and 1979) against those of all immigrants. The percentage of recent immigrants who completed high school was 59 percent, compared to 53 percent for all immigrants; the percentage with a college degree was 16 percent for all immigrants, but 24 percent for recent immigrants. According to Portes and Rumbaut, "The view that the educational level of immigration has been declining over time does not find support in the data, either in terms of general averages or when disaggregated by national origins" (p. 59) (see table 5).

Very recent research finds that whatever decline in immigrant skills and education levels has taken place was reversed in the mid– and late 1980s. For example, Funkhouser and Trejo (1993) find a marked improvement in education

Table 5. Educational Attainment of Immigrant Groups,* 1980

Country of Birth	High School Graduates (percent)	Completed 4 Years or More of College (percent)	Immigrated 1975–1980 (percent)
Nigeria	96.7	48.7	68.6
Taiwan	89.1	59.8	54.6
India	88.9	66.2	43.7
Egypt	87.3	50.2	32.4
Iran	87.1	42.8	71.9
Australia	81.0	27.6	28.7
Israel	78.8	34.9	34.1
Peru	77.3	20.3	31.7
England	74.6	16.4	14.3
France	74.3	22.8	13.9
Argentina	70.9	24.2	25.2
Netherlands	67.6	20.3	8.3
Germany	67.3	14.9	6.3
United States	**66.5**	**16.2**	**n.a.**
Colombia	62.8	14.6	29.6
Canada	61.8	14.3	9.8
Soviet Union	47.2	15.7	21.1
Guatemala	42.7	6.9	40.1
El Salvador	41.4	6.5	51.3
Yugoslavia	41.1	10.2	7.4
Greece	40.4	9.5	12.9
Laos	32.2	6.5	97.2
Dominican Republic	30.1	4.3	31.0
Italy	28.6	5.3	4.0
Portugal	22.3	3.3	21.7
Mexico	21.3	3.0	33.0

* aged twenty-five years or older.

Sources: Bureau of the Census, *Socioeconomic Characteristics of the US Foreign-Born Population Detailed in the Census Bureau Tabulations,* Release CB84-179. Washington, DC: US Department of Commerce, 1984, tables 1 and 2; Alejandro Portes and Ruben G. Rumbaut, *Immigrant America.* Berkeley: University of California Press, 1990, 60–61.

levels for the immigrants who arrived between 1987 and 1989. They find that the percentage of recently arrived immigrants who had less than eight years of schooling was 33 percent in 1979, but had decreased to 23 percent in 1989. More important, the percentage of recent immigrants with a college degree increased from 19 percent in 1979 to 26 percent in 1989. Not surprisingly, Funkhouser and Trejo also find a marked increase in the wages of the immigrants who came in the late 1980s, with earnings about 20 percent higher than for those who came in the early 1980s (when controlled for the length of time in the United States). They attribute much of the improvement in immigrant skills and education levels in the late 1980s to a resurgence of European immigration:

> Reversing a trend which dates back to the 1930s, the share of immigrants originating in Europe rose dramatically during the 1980s, with this surge being accommodated by reduced immigration from Latin America especially Mexico.

Elaine Sorenson and Maria Enchautegui (1992) of the Urban Institute also have verified that immigrant quality actually increased in the 1980s. They find that the immigrants who arrived between 1985 and 1989 had higher education levels than the immigrants who arrived in the 1970s. Sorenson insists, "The level of education of recent immigrants has definitely increased over the last 10 years" (quoted in Mandel and Farrell 1992, 116).

The data on average education and earnings that are often cited to suggest a dramatic decline in immigrant quality camouflage a critical point about the recent immigrants: Immigrants tend to be bimodal in skills and education. In other words, a disproportionate percentage of immigrants have low skills and/or education levels compared to US workers, but an almost equally disproportionate share are very highly skilled and/or educated. For example, according to Sorenson and Enchautegui (1992), more than one-quarter of the 1985–89 immigrants were college graduates, a higher percentage than among adult workers born in the United States. Similarly, occupation data from the US Department of Labor (1989) reveals that more than one-quarter of the 1985–87 immigrants were classified as "managerial or professional," the highest skill classification. This, too, is slightly higher than the percentage for US–born workers. In sum, the United States is attracting a large percentage of very highly skilled and very highly educated immigrants—and more so now than ever before.

Of course, the reverse is also true: the United States is receiving more low-skilled immigrants (relative to the skill levels of US–born workers) than in previous decades. Yet, as discussed above, there is no evidence that these low-skilled immigrants harm US workers through job competition or that they harm US taxpayers by drawing excessively on the welfare system. In fact, the occupational data shows that a very large percentage of immigrants are employed in the service industry—positions for which US workers are typically overqualified. Hence, the current inflow of immigrants may complement the skills of the US–born workforce.

Another reason to suspect that the decline in immigrant quality, identified by Borjas and others, has been overblown is that the reduction in immigrants' skill levels and earnings appear to be offset by other positive attributes of recent arrivals. Borjas (1990) concludes that the quality of recent immigrants has fallen based on assessments of their earnings, education, and so forth at the time of their arrival. However, Robert LaLonde and Robert Topel (1991) of the University of Chicago find that this analysis ignores the economic assimilation rate of immigrants, as measured by earnings growth from the time of entry into the United States. This point is important enough to elaborate. According to LaLonde and Topel (1991):

> Since immigrants assimilate with time in the United States, the decline in new immigrants' *initial* earnings capacity overstates the long term decline in immigrant quality. Further, those groups with the largest initial earnings disadvantage assimilate the most. Thus, an increase in the shares of Asians and Mexicans among new immigrants reduces new immigrants' relative earnings, but increases the average rate of assimilation . . .
>
> Europeans who arrived between 1965 and 1969 experienced no relative earnings growth at all during the 1970s, but they also started from parity in 1969. By comparison, Asians and Mexicans experienced relative earnings growth of 24 and 20 percent over the decade, respectively. Since Asians and Mexicans accounted for vastly larger proportions of new immigrants in the 1970s and 1980s, the rate of convergence between immigrant and native earnings will be correspondingly larger than in the past.

LaLonde and Topel suggest that after about ten years, almost all of the earnings and educational disadvantages of more recent immigrants relative to earlier immigrants disappear. They conclude, "We think that fears about declining immigrant quality have been exaggerated."

Economists Harriet Orcutt Duleep of the Urban Institute and Mark C. Regets (1992) have come independently to the same conclusion. They find that among recent immigrants—those who entered in the 1970s—there is a "systematic inverse relationship between initial earnings and the growth rate in earnings," and "the increased rate of growth [in earnings] greatly ameliorates the effect of lower entry wages on the lifetime earnings of immigrants." One reason that immigrants have lower initial earnings but experience a rapid path of economic assimilation is that new immigrants tend to originate from Asia and Central America, which means that a smaller percentage than in the past possess English-language skills at the time of entry (Duleep and Regets 1992). This lack of English proficiency would be expected to depress initial earnings, but earnings would be expected to accelerate once English skills are attained.

The argument that the quality of immigrants is declining is most directly refuted by examination of the human capital characteristics of recent ethnic groups that have immigrated to the United States. For example, what is most new about America's "new immigrants" is that they are largely Asian. As discussed above, the major shift in the origin of immigrants has been that Asian immigration has expanded to comprise nearly half the total. The 1990 census reveals that largely because of immigration, Asians are the fastest-growing minority in America; their population grew by 80 percent in the 1980s alone. Moreover, much of Americans' hostility toward the new immigrants is targeted specifically toward Asians. Therefore, any decline in immigrant quality would have to be apparent in a comparison of Asian immigrants to European immigrants. But it is not. In general, Asians have performed extraordinarily well (Dunn 1990; Kotkin 1992). For example:

- Asians have the highest earnings of any ethnic group in America. The household income of Asians was $36,100 in 1990, fully 25 percent higher than the $28,910 US average.

- Asians are America's most highly educated group. In 1989, about 40 percent of Asians were college graduates, compared to the 25 percent US average.

- Asians tend to be overrepresented in the highest levels of scholarship. They are two-and-a-half times more likely than US–born adults to have postgraduate degrees. Whereas Asians comprise only 3 percent of the US population, they comprise 20 percent of the Harvard class of 1994.

Of course, some Asian groups fare better than others. Immigrants from India, for example, have almost one-and-a-half more years of schooling than the average American. Portes and Rumbaut (1990) report that in 1980, the average

Indian family income was more than $6,000 above the average US income, even though 80 percent of these immigrants had been in the United States less than ten years, that is, they were "new immigrants."

Another new immigrant group that has prospered has been Arabs. The 1980 census reveals that the average Arab family income exceeds the US average by almost 10 percent. More than three-fourths of the two million Arab-Americans have high school degrees, compared to only two-thirds of US born adults (Toth 1991, A5).

In short, the social assimilation and economic progress of the Asians who have immigrated over the last three decades has been an astounding American success story. According to Kevin McCarthy, coauthor of the 1985 RAND Corporation study on the impact of immigrants on the California economy, Asians are "the most highly skilled of any immigrant group we've ever had" (quoted in Holden 1989, 290). Kotkin (1992) comes to almost precisely the same conclusion in his study of the economic assimilation and traits of various ethnic groups in America. Kotkin concludes: "Taken together, Asians constitute arguably the most talented, commercially oriented large group since the massive influx of Jews in the early part of the twentieth century" (p. 110).

Two final points need to be emphasized about the quality of recent immigrants vis-à-vis the Europeans who arrived during earlier decades. First, even if we accept the proposition that there has been some undesirable deterioration in immigrant quality for some ethnic groups—what appears to be driving down average skill and education levels is that Mexicans are coming with less human capital than previously—it would be wrong to conclude that these immigrants are undesirable. As economist Julian Simon (1990) points out, there is no evidence that the new immigrants are not a net benefit to the US economy; there is only some evidence that they are *less of a benefit than earlier arrivals.* The key economic determinant is whether immigrants raise the average income level of Americans, and there is substantial evidence (presented in the following section) that even low-skilled immigrants do.

The second point to be emphasized is that the problem of declining immigrant quality is easily solved: the United States can, in short, recruit all of the high-skilled immigrants it desires by expanding the system now in place to admit immigrants based on their skills. The Immigration Act of 1990 did increase the percentage of skills-tested immigrants from about 5 percent of the total to about 10 percent. Table 6 shows that skills testing has been a very successful way to recruit talented immigrants. Roughly six of ten of these immigrants during 1985–87 were in managerial and professional occupations (the highest earnings category)—twice the percentage for native-born Americans. Yet, there is a long

Table 6. Occupations of Immigrants and US Citizens, 1985–1987

	All US Workers[a] (percent)	All Immigrants[b] (percent)	Skills-tested Immigrants[b] (percent)
Managerial and professional[c]	24	25	59
Technical, sales, and administrative	31	16	8
Production, craft, and repair	12	12	8
Operators and laborers	16	22	2
Service occupations	13	20	22
Agricultural work	3	5	1
Total	99	100	100

a.   1987
b.   1985–87
c.   Includes managers, executives, architects, engineers, doctors, lawyers, teachers, and computer scientists.

Source: US Department of Labor, Bureau of International Labor Affairs, *The Effects of Immigration on the US Economy and Labor Market,* Immigration Policy and Research Report 1. Washington, DC: US Government Printing Office, 1989.

list of highly skilled immigrants waiting for visas. If the United States were to reserve 20 percent of the total visas for skills-tested immigrants, the average education level of all incoming immigrants would rise *above* the average for all US adults by one year, and the percentage of immigrants with at least one year of college would be 10 percent higher than for all US adults (Moore 1990c, 8). That is, these immigrants would have the educational attainment levels that employers will be seeking in the next century.

Harvard economist John Kenneth Galbraith writes:

We all look back with favor on our past immigrants and what they have done for us. It is deeply inconsistent that we think the future to be different. Why is it that what has proven so beneficial in the past should be questioned in the future?" (quoted in Moore 1990b)

The case that US immigration policy should be more restrictive because of declining immigrant skill levels is uncompelling. Although there is some cause for concern, the "new immigrants" have other positive characteristics, including very high levels of entrepreneurship and high rates of economic assimilation, which appear to more than compensate for the lower initial skills and earnings disadvantages. The eventual success of recent immigrants in the marketplace suggests that they are among the most beneficial ever to come to the United States. Complaints that the new immigrants are worse than the old are as invalid today as they were when the Supreme Court used them to uphold the barriers to Chinese immigration a hundred years ago.

Policy Recommendation

America can and should provide greater opportunities for entry of highly skilled immigrants who can make substantial and immediate economic contributions. The number of skills-tested visas should be substantially expanded. *This should be done in addition to, rather than as a substitute for, the current family immigration preferences.* An additional 100,000 to 200,000 visas should be available each year through a selection system whereby points are awarded on the basis of education level, occupational skills, English-language proficiency, and perhaps other characteristics. Visas should be awarded to the immigrants with the highest point totals each year. Under such a system, about 20 to 30 percent of immigrant visas would be awarded on the basis of skills, up from less than 10 percent today. With this change, the people who immigrate to the United States in the 1990s and into the next century will be the most talented ever to come.

6

Immigration and US Cities

At the Lower East Side Jewish Festival yesterday, a Chinese woman ate a pizza slice in front of Ty Thuan Duc's Vietnamese grocery store. Beside her a Spanish-speaking family patronized a cart with two signs: "Italian Ices" and "Kosher by Rabbi Alper." And after the pastrami ran out, everybody ate knishes. *(New York Times* 1987, cited in Rumbaut 1991).

T he principal reason for focusing on local labor markets," declares Harvard's Richard Freeman, "is that immigrants are concentrated by geographic area, constituting large and increasing proportions of the work force in 'gateway cities' but negligible proportions elsewhere" (Freeman and Abowd 1990). Today, roughly three-quarters of the immigrants who arrived in the 1980s settled in just six states: California, Florida, Illinois, New Jersey, New York, and Texas. Over half of all immigrants reside in just a handful of cities, including Los Angeles, New York, Chicago, Miami, San Diego, and Houston.

Understanding the local impact of immigrants is critical to any national debate on immigration policy for three reasons. First, America's cities have a rich, proud, and continuing history not only as the nation's industrial centers, but also as repositories of its cultural and intellectual heritage. Since cities are of special importance to America, we need to know how immigrants are influencing them. Second, immigrants' economic and social impact should be most easily observed on the local level, within the metropolitan labor markets where they live and work. A final reason to investigate the local impact of immigrants is that in recent years opponents of immigration have argued that immigrants are rapidly changing the face of America's cities in ways that Americans might find deeply disturbing.

Newspapers report scary statistics about whites in Texas cities becoming a minority by the middle of the next century because of "mass migration." *Newsweek* recently raised the alarm for Californians with a frightening headline: "Los Angeles 2010: A Latino Subcontinent" (quoted in Myer 1992, 32). The article predicts that within a generation, "California will be demographically, culturally, and economically distinct from the rest of America." Gordon J. McDonald, former head of the US Border Patrol, is even more blunt in his assessment of the urban impact of immigrants: "Major cities have already been turned into extensions of foreign countries. Aliens threaten to seize political power within a few short years" (quoted in Fossedal 1990a). Daniel James, author of *Illegal Immigration: An Unfolding Crisis,* says of California's immigrants: "The frightening prospect is that there will never be enough money to rescue California from insolvency as long as millions of immigrants keep pouring in uninterruptedly" (James 1992).

It is undeniable that many of America's once-great industrial centers in the Northeast and Midwest are in decline. It would be natural to believe that the continuous influx of immigrants is a principal cause. The decline of America's cities is evident in statistics on rising crime rates, increasing poverty levels, job losses, business closings, and the out-migration of the white middle class (Moore 1993). Over the past twenty years, fifteen of the most highly populated US cities lost nearly four million people, a remarkably large exodus given that over this same time period the US population grew by more than fifty million (Moore 1993). Meanwhile, many major cities suffer severe fiscal crises with unprecedented levels of taxation and service cuts.

But immigrants are not primarily responsible for this urban "sclerosis." In fact, they are a primary catalyst for rebuilding and revitalizing America's inner cities. Without immigration, urban decline would be far more severe.

One of the most significant benefits of immigration is that it has offset the out-migration of workers and businesses from inner cities. Table 7 shows that the populations of eight major US cities that grew by 5 percent in the 1980s would have *fallen* by almost 7 percent without immigration. Immigration is preventing catastrophic population declines in major US cities. Critics of immigration counter that Americans are leaving the cities precisely because foreigners are entering them—immigrants allegedly makes urban areas less desirable places in which to live (Filer 1988). In an analysis of data from the 1980 and 1985 Current Population Surveys, Butcher and Card (1991) find that

Table 7. Impact of Immigration on Population Growth in Selected US Cities, 1980–1990

	Change in the Number of Residents	
	Immigrants (thousands)	US Citizens (thousands)
Boston	+ 60	- 50
Chicago	+210	-430
Houston	+170	-135
Los Angeles	+755	-240
Miami	+105	- 90
New York	+955	-705
San Francisco	+160	- 85
Seattle	+ 30	- 10

Source: Michael Mandel and Christopher Farrell, "The Immigrants: How They're Helping to Revitalize the US Economy," *Business Week,* 13 July 1992, 115–16.

native population growth rates in cities and immigration levels into cities may be *positively correlated* (p. 292). When they examine population growth rates for twenty-four major US cities, they discover that immigration has neither a positive nor a negative effect on native population growth. However, when they exclude the three most immigrant-intensive cities—Los Angeles, Miami, and New York—they find that each additional immigrant led to an increase of 1.76 US-born residents into the city. Americans are not leaving cities because of the presence of immigrants.

The economic growth rates of US cities appear, on balance, to be positively associated with immigration. I recently compiled an economic index of the eighty largest US cities for the period 1965–90 (see Moore 1993), which takes into account four economic growth measures: change in population, change in employment, change in per capita income, and change in the poverty rate. Then I examined the foreign-born population in the ten fastest-growing and slowest-growing cities according to 1990 Census Bureau data. The results, shown in table 8, should dispel any notion that immigration is a *cause* of urban decline: in the ten fastest-growing cities, the foreign-born constitute 17.9 percent of the resident population; in the ten slowest-growing cities, the foreign-born constitute 6.8 percent of the population. In other words, high-growth cities have more than twice as many immigrants as low-growth cities. To be sure, this nonscientific evidence does not prove that immigrants cause economic growth in cities, but it does strongly suggest that the decline of central cities and the high poverty rates there are caused by factors other than immigration. Detroit, Cleveland, Philadelphia, Buffalo, and St. Louis—among our most economically and financially troubled cities—all have very small immigrant populations.

Several scientific studies have documented what my casual evidence implies, namely that immigration and economic growth of cities are positively correlated. For example, a comprehensive study of the impact of immigrants on cities between 1970 and 1980 by economist Richard Freeman finds evidence that job growth and immigration were positively related:

> There is some evidence that cities with more immigrants, employ-
> ment grew more rapidly or declined more slowly in low wage
> industries where immigrants tended to find jobs and that less skilled
> natives moved into better jobs. The broad implication is that immi-
> grants have been absorbed into the American labor market with little
> adverse effect on natives. (Freeman and Abowd 1990)

In our recent study (Vedder, Galloway, and Moore, 1990), we show that immigration is positively associated with labor-force participation rates by state. (The labor-force participation rate is an important component of economic growth, because growth rates can be raised only by increases in the factors of production—labor and capital—or by technological improvements.) We use data on labor-force participation rates from 1982 to 1985 for the forty-eight continental states as the dependent variable, and the percentage of the state's population that is foreign-born in 1980 as the independent variable, along with several other factors that might account for interstate variations in labor-force participation rates. These include the number of people who receive public assistance and the size of the population receiving Social Security. We find that holding these other factors constant, immigration has a statistically significant positive effect on labor-force participation rates. A 1 percent rise in the proportion of a state's population that is foreign-born raises the labor-force participation rate by 0.19 percentage points. This means that states with higher

Table 8. Immigrant Populations in High- and Low-Growth US Cities, 1965–1990

	Foreign-Born Population (percent)
Ten Highest-Growth Cities (average)	**17.9**
San Jose, CA	26.5
Charlotte, NC	3.8
Santa Ana, CA	50.9
Las Vegas, NV	10.3
Anaheim, CA	28.4
Riverside, CA	15.5
Phoenix, AZ	8.6
Austin, TX	8.6
Albuquerque, NM	5.5
San Diego, CA	20.9
Ten Lowest-Growth Cities (average)	**6.8**
Detroit, MI	3.4
Rochester, NY	6.2
Buffalo, NY	4.5
Milwaukee, WI	4.7
Louisville, KY	1.5
Chicago, IL	16.9
St. Louis, MO	2.5
Philadelphia, PA	6.6
Cincinnati, OH	2.8
Newark, NJ	18.7

Sources: Foreign-born populations compiled by Rick Swartz & Associates, Washington, DC, based on 1990 census data; city rankings based on Stephen Moore, "The Myth of America's Underfunded Cities," *Policy Analysis*, Washington, DC: Cato Institute, 1993.

proportions of immigration, such as Florida and California, over time can be expected to experience more rapid growth in per capita income than low-immigration states, such as Iowa and West Virginia.

In its comprehensive report on immigration and US labor markets, the US Department of Labor (1989) came to a similarly benign conclusion on the local and regional impact of immigration. This exhaustive study of more than fifty area-wide labor market studies concludes:

> Research within specific metropolitan areas and regional labor markets reveals some substitution/displacement [of natives] occurring in some low skilled occupations, although beneficial effects are also observed. Regional studies do not support claims of disproportionate effects of immigration on any particular region . . . .
>
> The economic recovery of New York City in the 1980s and the continued vitality of Los Angeles and Miami have been fueled by voluminous increases in small business activity. Immigrants are directly responsible for a substantial share of this activity. (p. 94)

Evidence for the three most heavily impacted cities—Los Angeles, Miami, and New York—further confirms this conclusion.

Los Angeles

In no city has the economy and culture been shaped by recent immigrant waves more than in Los Angeles. In 1980, about 1.7 million immigrants lived in the city, but by 1990, that number had approached 2 million (Muller and Espenshade 1985). Immigrants now constitute about one-sixth of the city's population. More important, immigrants accounted for about 70 percent of the growth of the city's labor force in the 1970s, a trend that continued in the 1980s (US Department of Labor 1989, 73).

It is also true that in no city has immigration been more controversial. Critics of immigration maintain that the large size of the immigrant flow into Los Angeles, and its predominantly Hispanic and Asian character, are contributing to racial tensions in the city. According to some analysts, immigration may even have helped spark the Los Angeles riots in 1992 (James 1992.) Low-skilled, inner-city blacks in Los Angeles are said to harbor resentment against immigrants, against whom they compete for scarce jobs.

Yet major research finds a strongly positive economic impact of immigration on the California economy. For example, the Urban Institute's landmark study (Muller and Espenshade 1985) found that Los Angeles prospered in the 1970s in part because of large economic contributions of immigrants. For example, even with a huge inflow of Mexican manufacturing workers, employment in Los Angeles for black teenagers and adults increased at rates faster than the national average through the 1970s and early 1980s. Black wages also rose faster than the national average over the same period.

Blacks were not the only beneficiaries of the large immigrant flow. The study found that despite the addition of 220,000 new Mexican immigrants during the 1970s, unemployment rates in the city *fell* relative to the nationwide rate and per capita income rose faster. Manufacturing jobs in Los Angeles grew at an astounding rate—four times the national rate—with immigrants filling from a third to half of the new positions. In fact, an estimated one-quarter of the jobs filled by Mexican immigrants would have disappeared, and the apparel industry would have migrated south of the Mexican border, according to Muller and Espenshade (1985), if immigrant workers had not been available. Finally, for California consumers, Mexican immigration meant lower prices for many goods and services and less inflation than experienced by the nation as a whole. "The bottom line consensus on the impact of Mexican immigrants on Los Angeles is that, on balance, they are an economic benefit," say Muller and Espenshade.

Another analysis of Mexican immigrants in California, by the RAND Corporation (McCarthy and Valdez 1985), reached similar conclusions. It compares 1970 and 1980 US census data on demographic, employment, and earnings changes for California, and finds that: "widespread concerns about Mexican immigrants are generally unfounded. Overall, the immigrants have provided strong economic benefits for the state, with only minor dislocation effects, mostly among native-born Latinos." It further concludes that immigrants' "use of public services in general is not a problem," although it finds that Los Angeles and other heavily impacted cities had to bear a "disproportionate cost burden while receiving a less-than-proportionate share of the tax revenues." Finally, the study dismisses the idea that recent immigrants have failed to assimilate into the local and state economy as is commonly charged: "Mexican immigrants are not fostering a separate society. They are integrating into the state's society as other immigrants have done."

Miami

Miami's economy and social institutions have been markedly transformed over the past three decades in large part because of a heavy influx of Cubans fleeing the regime of Fidel Castro. With more than 450,000 new immigrants settling in Miami's Dade County in the 1980s alone, Miami has been called "the new Ellis Island." Hispanics today constitute about half the county's population, but more than one in three Miami residents is an immigrant—higher than the 1 to 4 foreign-born ratio in Los Angeles and far higher than the ratio in any other major US city.

Miami is a case study in how even very heavy immigration and rapid economic progress can be largely compatible. In a study of the impact of immigrants on US cities, economists Demetrious Papademetriou and Thomas Muller (1987) conclude that the result of three decades of heavy immigration from Cuba has allowed Miami to develop "into a modern, advanced, city with dynamic economic linkages to Latin America." This is in large part attributable to the entrepreneurial talents of the Cubans who came in the 1970s and 1980s. Portes and Bach (1985) find that one-fifth of the Cuban immigrants who arrived between 1973 and 1979 either owned or operated a business or professional service during that period. Today, there are an estimated 25,000 Cuban-owned businesses in Miami *(Economist,* 11 May 1991, 20). Statistics indicate that the family income of the 1960–80 Cuban immigrants is higher than the average for US families.

Nineteen-eighty was the year of the Mariel boatlift. In less than eighteen months, 125,000 Mariel Cubans traveled to Miami, and it is estimated that over half of those exiles stayed. This surge in immigrant workers represented a 7 percent increase in the Miami labor force overnight. If immigrants do cause unemployment for US workers; if immigrants do lower wages; if immigrants do harm the economic opportunities of blacks; if immigrants do destroy the social fabric of a local area, then one would certainly expect to observe evidence of these effects in Miami following the influx of the Mariel Cubans. A major study of the impact of the Mariel boatlift on the Miami economy six years afterwards by Princeton economist David Card (1990) found few such adverse effects. Card's conclusion is worth repeating:

> The influx of Mariel Cubans had virtually no effect on the wage rates of less-skilled non-Cuban workers. Similarly there is no evidence of an increase in unemployment among less skilled blacks or other non-Cuban workers. Rather the data analysis suggests a remarkably rapid absorption of the Mariel immigrants into the Miami labor force, with negligible effects on other groups. Even among the Cuban population there is no evidence that wages or unemployment rates of earlier arrivals were substantially affected by the arrival of the Mariels. (p. 256)

These findings are important in understanding how immigrants integrate into local areas. Card's study demonstrates that local labor markets are often remarkably adaptive and resilient. That Miami was able to absorb a 7 percent increase in its labor force with almost no observable negative impact in terms of unemployment, wages, or minority employment opportunities, suggests that we need not worry about the absorptive capacities of most US cities, which rarely experience annual immigrant flows of one-tenth that magnitude.

New York

Joel Kotkin (1992) notes that New York "is a city whose economic history has been shaped by repeated waves of entrepreneurial immigrants" (p. 110). In the 1920s, more than two-thirds of New Yorkers were either immigrants or children of immigrants, and the situation is not much different today (Levinew 1990). More than two million foreign-born now live in the New York metropolitan area. In fact, the infusion during the 1970s and 1980s of Koreans, Chinese, Indians, Vietnamese, Mexicans, Jamaicans, and others has meant that the city's population has stayed fairly constant at between seven and eight million people. Without the immigrants, the population of New would have declined spectacularly to less than six million *(Economist,* 11 May 1991, 20).

The modern-day immigrants have provided a new lease on life for many declining industries and many depressed areas of the city. For example, Koreans have come to dominate small-scale retailing in New York—businesses ranging from corner delicatessens to fruit and vegetable stores. The Chinese in the vibrant Chinatown section of lower Manhattan have revitalized the city's garment industry and increasingly own and operate some of the most successful mid-sized banks (Kotkin 1992, 11).

One reason recent immigrants have prospered in New York is that they bring with them skills and investment capital. Aaron Gurwitz (1991), a vice-president at Goldman Sachs in New York, finds that the current immigrant waves are extraordinarily successful economically:

Table 9. Economic and Social Characteristics of American-Born and Foreign-Born in New York City, 1980

	American-Born (percent)	Foreign-Born (percent)
Labor-Force Participation		
Males	87.1	90.5
Females	60.9	61.9
Unemployment Rate		
Males	7.0	6.2
Females	6.6	7.6
Receiving Public Assistance	13.3	7.7
Crimes	87.3	12.7
Proportion of the Population	76.4	23.6

Source: Elizabeth Bogen, Testimony before the Joint Economic Committee, US Congress, *Hearings on the Economic and Demographic Consequences of Immigration.* Washington, DC: US Government Printing Office, 29 May 1986.

In contrast with the groups that came to the United States during the period between 1880 and 1920, the recent immigrants are better educated and wealthier. Previous immigration waves have provided New York City employers with a motivated, though not necessarily highly skilled work force. This generation of immigrants tends to be much better educated, and in many cases, to bring with them enough capital to start a new business.

In 1986, the New York City Department of Immigration Services compared immigrants and US–born New Yorkers on a whole range of social and economic statistics, including welfare usage, labor market characteristics, and crime rates. The results, shown in table 9, indicate that the foreign born in New York have higher labor-force participation rates, lower rates of public assistance utilization, lower crime rates, and roughly equal unemployment rates (Bogen 1986). The report concludes:

New York City seems well able to absorb immigrants at the rate at which they are now entering the city. There seems to be room for them in the job market, in the institutional structure, and in the infrastructure . . . . Immigrants do pose some problems to this city, *but the balance is unquestionably favorable.* (Bogen 1986; emphasis added)

Policy Recommendation

Immigrants are revitalizing America's cities and are a net economic benefit to the regions where they live and work. There is no reason to reduce immigration because of the effect on high-immigrant cities and states. Even accounting for the fact that immigrants use mostly local services but pay mostly federal taxes, in the long run immigrants are a good deal for the cities and states where they live. For this reason, legislation that would reimburse states and cities for the cost of public services used by immigrants are misguided.

One step the federal government should take to help the fiscal situation of high-immigrant cities and states would be to restrict AFDC and Medicaid eligibility to US–born citizens—or at least to deny benefits to immigrants for their first five years in the United States. This would ease the fiscal burden on states, which now pick up half the cost of AFDC and Medicaid. The federal government should also consider establishing a $2,500 federally funded education voucher program for immigrant children. The voucher could be used to send immigrant children to a public or private school.

7

Why America Still Needs Immigrants

The empires of the future, are the empires of the mind.
— Winston Churchill

Each of the preceding sections has been primarily a refutation of common myths about the economic costs of immigration to the United States. The evidence is compelling that immigrants are not a drain on the American economy. But this does not answer the question of why the United States should continue to accept immigration at all? In this section, I make an affirmative case for a liberal immigration policy by highlighting the economic benefits of immigrants.

Immigration and the High-Technology Frontier

In the 1980s, the United States assumed world leadership in many high-technology industries, including computer design and software, pharmaceuticals, health care technology, electronics, robotics, and aerospace engineering, among others. This leadership position has been significantly enhanced by the presence in the United States of foreign-born talent. It is not uncommon to find highly profitable firms in the nation's high-tech corridors, from Route 128 in Massachusetts to Silicon Valley in California, that employ more immigrants than US–born workers. British, Taiwanese, Korean, Indian, Filipino, and Cuban scientists are the lifeblood of some of America's most successful high-tech firms (Moore 1991).

No company illustrates this point better than Intel Corporation, which recorded more than $1. 1 billion in profits in 1992. Three members of its top management are immigrants, including founder and CEO Andrew S. Grove. Some its most successful and revolutionary computer technologies were pioneered by immigrants, such as the 8080 microprocessor (an expanded-power computer chip), which was invented by a Japanese; and polysilicon FET gates (the basic unit of memory storage on modern computer chips), invented by an Italian. Dick Ward, manager of Intel's training program, says:

> Our whole business is predicated on inventing the next generation of computer technologies. The engine that drives that quest is brain-power. And here at Intel, much of that brainpower comes from immigrants. (Interview with author, October 1990)

At Du Pont Merck Pharmaceutical Co., an $800 million a year health-care products firm based in Wilmington, Delaware, immigrants are responsible for many of the company's most promising new product innovations. For example, Losartan, an anti-hypertensive drug, was developed by a team of scientists that included two Chinese immigrants and a Lithuanian (Mandell and Farrell 1992, 117). Joseph Mollica, president of Du Pont Merck, says that bringing together talent from different cultures and backgrounds means diversity of insight that "lets you look at problems and opportunities from a slightly different point of view" (Mandel and Farrell 1992, 117).

At the high-growth International Paper Company in Hawthorne, New York, 60 percent of the Operations Analysis and Engineering Department are immigrants (Moore 1991, 47). One of the firm's most productive research teams consists of immigrants from Turkey, Israel, Philippines, Egypt, India, Taiwan, and Uruguay.

A final example is Cypress Semiconductor Corporation in San Jose, California, the thirteenth-largest semiconductor company in the United States, with sales of $250 million in 1992. The firm's vice-president for research is a refugee from Cuba. Its two most outstanding technicians, responsible for new product development, are from India and Mexico. The firm's president and founder, T. J. Rodgers, says that Cypress is "critically dependent on immigrants ranging from semi-skilled assembly line workers to top technical people" (interview with author, March 1993).

Intel, Du Pont Merck, International Paper, and Cypress Semiconductor are not unique in their reliance on immigration. Robert Kelley, Jr., president of SO/CAL/TEN, an association of nearly 200 California high-tech firms, insists that "Without the influx of Asians in the 1980s, we would not have had the entrepreneurial explosion we've seen in California" (quoted in Kotkin 1989, 24). David N. K. Wang, vice-president of Applied Materials Inc., a California-based computer-technology firm, adds, "Silicon Valley is one of the most international business centers in the world" (Hof 1992, 120). The numbers confirm this assessment. There are currently well over 15,000 Asian immigrants employed in Silicon Valley alone *(Economist,* 27 January 1990). This is roughly one-fourth of the workforce in that high-tech capital (Barkan 1989, 55). More than 10,000 of these Asians are Chinese or Indian. At IBM's facility in Yorktown Heights, NY, one-fourth of the researchers are Asian. At AT&T's world-re-nowned Bell Labs, 40 percent of the scientists are first- or second-generation Asian immigrants (Kotkin 1992, 108).

An even more heartening success story is that of Phoenix Laser Systems, in San Jose, California. The founder and director of research for this cutting-edge medical laser firm is Alfred Sklar, a Cuban immigrant who escaped Castro in the 1960s. Sklar is recognized as the central brain of a pioneering effort to perfect laser and surgical technologies that could cure several forms of blindness and could eventually revolutionize optical surgery in the United States and through-out the world. Sklar has been touted by the *Wall Street Journal* as one of America's "brilliant scientists . . . challenging the laser industry with radically new machines that could prove cheaper, safer, and more accurate than more common laser approaches" (1990).

New research is beginning to quantify the contributions of immigrants to America's leading technology-driven industries. One of the most comprehensive studies on the impact of the foreign-born on America's scientific industries was conducted by the National Research Council (1988), which finds:

> A survey of the R&D directors of 20 firms that account for a large fraction of the technological output of the United States indicated that their particular industries are, in fact, dependent upon foreign talent and that such dependency is growing. Several respondents stated that "foreign talent was a critical element of the firm's operations."

Thus, it is clear . . . that these foreign-born engineers enrich our culture and make substantial contributions to the US economic well-being and competitiveness and that without the use of noncitizen and foreign-born engineers, universities and industries would experience difficulty in staffing current educational, research, development, and technological programs.

Few would dispute that America's international competitiveness in the next century will be closely tied to the nation's ability to retain its world leadership in high-growth, capital-intensive industries. The US ability to do so is linked closely to its continued ability to attract and retain highly talented workers from abroad.

Immigrant Scientists, Engineers, and Scholars

International leadership in science, technology, and basic R&D is not dictated by the quantity of scientists and researchers as much as by their quality. A few highly creative innovators can create and capture entire new industries.

Immigrants to the United States are a source of large quantities of high-quality scientists, engineers, mathematicians, computer specialists, and medical specialists. For example, a 1990 *New York Times Magazine* article, entitled "In the Trenches of Science," discusses the discovery of superconductivity: a technology that is expected to spawn hundreds of vital new commercial applications in the next century (cited in Wattenberg 1991, 55–56). The scientist who discovered superconductivity is a physicist at the University of Houston, Ching-Wu Chu, who was born in China and came to the United States in 1972. He is a top contender for a Nobel prize.

American scientific and engineering prowess in the world today is in large part attributable to the influx of highly talented immigrants over the past three decades. In 1980, one of three engineers working in the United States was an immigrant (National Science Foundation 1986). Fifty-five percent of the doctoral degrees awarded in engineering at American universities in 1985 went to foreign-born students (National Science Foundation 1986). Throughout the 1980s, two out of five mathematics and computer science doctorates went to immigrant students, and according to the National Science Foundation, more than 80 percent of these students will stay and work for US firms.

The impact of these foreign scholars has been uniformly positive. According to the National Research Council (1988):

Very significant, positive aspects arise from the presence of foreign-born engineers in our society. It must be recognized that with these foreign engineers the United States is attracting an unusually gifted group of individuals with high intellectual competence and diligence. The diversity of intellectual backgrounds and experience that other foreign born engineers have brought in the past greatly contributed to US engineering competence, and there are no reasons to believe that new immigrants will not contribute similarly. (p. 3)

The study examined the issue of whether foreign-born engineers depress the wage rates of US–born engineers, and concludes that such a claim "is not supported by the evidence" (p. 3). It also finds that foreign-born graduates create a windfall for the US economy because "the dollar cost to the country for acquiring the services of these unusually gifted individuals is relatively low, substantially less than the real cost of bringing a US citizen to the same level of training and performance."

Brookings Institution scholars J. Lerner and R. Roy (1984) have examined the quality of these immigrant scientists and engineers. They uncover solid evidence that a large number of the most outstanding scientific scholars in the world are immigrants living in the United States. For example, they find that immigrants are overrepresented among the memberships of the National Academy of Engineering and the National Academy of Sciences. They also find that between 1901 and 1982, "immigrant engineers/scientists constitute between 20 and 50 percent of the Nobel prize winners, depending on the discipline involved." In sum, if Ching-Wu Chu does win a Nobel prize for superconductivity he will join a long list of US winners who are immigrants.

Lerner and Roy (1984) attempt to quantify the value of the education transferred to the United States through the immigration of scientists and engineers. They find that the total value to the United States of these immigrants from 1950 to 1975 is roughly equivalent to an annual net flow of capital to the United States of as much as $8. 6 billion (p. 250). This was more than the total amount of US foreign aid to the Third World over this period. Lerner and Roy summarize their findings:

From the very visible presence of foreign physicians in all major city hospital staffs to the Nobel prize winners imported to these shores, this unplanned—yet enormously significant—immigration strategy has played a significant role in building the technical personnel base of the US.

Many of these scholars also contribute significantly to the cultivation of US–born talent. It is almost certain that US–born engineering and science students benefit from competing against the top analytical minds from around the world. Moreover, the recruitment and retention of foreign faculty is essential to maintaining the high standards of US institutions of higher education. William Kirwan (1990), president of the University of Maryland, College Park, explains:

> In order to prepare the current generation of college students for leadership roles in private industry and government, academic institutions must have access to the very best faculty members from this nation and across the world. American universities have traditionally recruited a small but critical number of world-class teaching faculty from abroad.

Our children's economic future will be richer if the gates are kept wide open to such scholars.

Immigrants as Entrepreneurs

One of the most favorable characteristics of immigrants is their high propensity to start new businesses. Table 10 shows the rate of new business start-ups and the gross sales of such firms by ethnic groups in 1982, and indicates that some immigrant groups are much more likely to start new businesses than are natives. For example, according to Portes and Rumbaut (1990), "In Los Angeles, the propensity for self-employment is three times greater for Koreans than among the population as a whole. Grocery stores, restaurants, gas stations, liquor stores, and real estate offices are typical Korean businesses." Cubans also are prodigious creators of new businesses. The number of Cuban-owned firms in Miami has expanded from 919 in 1967, to 8,000 in 1976, to 28,000 in 1990 (*Economist,* 11 May 1991, 20). A final example: on Jefferson Boulevard in Dallas there are over 800 businesses operating today, three-quarters of which are owned and operated by first- and second-generation Hispanic immigrants (Mandel and Farrell 1992, 118). Just ten years ago, before the influx of Mexicans and other Central Americans, this neighborhood was in decay, with vacant stores and "for sale" signs; today, it is a thriving ethnic neighborhood.

It is undeniably true that, as with all new business start-ups, most immigrant establishments are small and marginally profitable. The average immigrant firm employs about four workers and records roughly $200,000 in annual sales

Table 10. Immigrant and Minority Firm Ownership and Performance, 1982

	Firms per 100,000 Population	Employees per Firm	Gross Receipts per Firm (thousands)
Mexican	275.9	4.4	$201.1
Cuban	638.2	4.3	$267.6
Central and South American	455.8	3.3	$181.7
Chinese	1,750.6	6.5	$351.7
Japanese	968.8	4.7	$293.0
Korean	2,223.4	3.1	$216.0
Filipino	391.7	2.7	$133.7
Indian	1,764.4	3.2	$176.2
Vietnamese	366.4	2.4	$131.8
American Black	145.8	4.3	$220.8

Sources: Bureau of the Census, *Survey of Minority-Owned Business Enterprises, 1982— Blacks, Hispanics, and Asian Americans,* Release MB82-1/3. Washington, DC: US Department of Commerce, 1985, table 1; Alejandro Portes and Ruben G. Rumbaut, *Immigrant America.* Berkeley: University of California Press, 1990, 76.

(Portes and Rumbaut 1990, 76). However, such small businesses are a significant source of jobs: from 1975 to 1985, more than one-quarter of all new jobs were created by firms with less than twenty workers.

The stereotype of immigrants running small neighborhood shops, corner groceries, and dry cleaning establishments obscures the vital fact that some immigrant firms, particularly in the scientific and high-technology industries, are extraordinarily successful and vital to US global competitiveness. A 1990 study by the Alexis de Tocqueville Institute surveys high-technology firms in Silicon Valley and finds that roughly one in four had been founded by immigrants—some 270 of them formed by Hong Kong and Mainland Chinese immigrants (cited in Fossedal 1990b). Many of them are highly profitable:

- Solectron, a San Jose circuit-board assembly company, is owned and operated by a Taiwanese immigrant. Sales have grown by an average of 50 percent each year over the past twelve years, totalling $180 million in 1991. It is one of the leading US companies successfully breaking the decade-long domination of Japanese and Korean companies in the area of computer design. In 1991, Solectron won the prestigious Malcolm Baldrige National Quality Award (Mandel and Farrell 1992).

- AST Research is a computer company in Irvine that was founded in 1972 by a Pakistani and two Chinese immigrants. Its first-year sales were barely $500,000; in 1992, sales were $500 million (Mandel and Farrell 1992).

- In 1983, two Vietnamese electronics technicians and a Chinese engineer launched Integrated Circuits, Inc., a computer-assembly firm in Los Angeles. By 1986, its sales exceeded $25 million, and it employed some 300 US workers (Mandel and Farrell 1992).

- American Megatrends, Inc., a designer of highly sophisticated computer software in Norcross, Georgia, was co-founded in 1985 by Subramonian Shankar, an immigrant computer engineer from India. In 1991, AMI boasted sales of $70 million. The company now employs 130 workers. "That is one good thing about America," observes Shankar. "If you are determined to succeed, there are ways to get it done" (quoted in Mandel and Farrell 1992).

One of the engines of entrepreneurial capitalism is risk-taking. The act of leaving one's homeland and immigrating to a new country and a different culture involves substantial risk. Indeed, this is part of the self-selection process that makes immigrants desirable. But immigrants also share other specific traits that contribute to their enterprising nature and their success in business. One is their tight community bonds. Within Asian communities, for example, various forms of highly efficient but informal community-based revolving credit arrangements have evolved, which allow immigrants to finance new enterprises (US Department of Labor 1989, 173). This is an Oriental custom that goes back many centuries. In Korean it is called *"kye,"* in Vietnamese, *"hui,"* and in Japanese, *"tanamoshi"* (Dunn 1990). This practice for financing small ethnic businesses is especially important because new immigrants typically lack access to conventional lenders. These kind of neighborhood-based business-financing arrangements are now being duplicated within black communities in New York, Washington, DC, and other cities.

Immigrants: The Best and the Brightest

It was said about the great wave of immigrants who came to America on steamships at the turn of the century that the cowardly stayed home and the weak died on the way. This meant that America was attracting a group of new citizens who tended to be highly motivated, resourceful, and enterprising. As James Fallows (1983) writes: "Looked at from the economic point of view, the immigrant's grit and courage, and even his anxieties, impart productive energy to the society he joins."

It is a romantic myth about the United States that the immigrants who come are, as Emma Lazarus put it in her famous poem, "poor, tired, and huddled masses." In fact, for more than a century, immigration has been a process by which America skims the cream of other nation's human capital.

Several studies have documented that the immigrants who come to the United States tend to be more skilled, more highly educated, wealthier, and generally more economically successful than the average citizen in their home countries. This is true of immigrants from both developed and Third World nations. A study by Ugalde, Bean, and Cardenas (1979) finds that Dominicans who immigrate to the United States are more likely to be literate, have higher skills, and be from the city—and for those who do come from rural areas, to be predominantly from large and medium-sized farms rather than from among the landless peasantry. Thomas Sowell (1981) of the Hoover Institute reports that black immigrants from the West Indies have far higher skill levels than their fellow countrymen who did not migrate (pp. 216–20). He also finds that the income levels of West Indian immigrants are higher than West Indian natives, higher than American blacks, and even higher than native-born white Americans. West Indian immigrants have been so successful that they have become known as "black Jews" (Sowell 1981, 219).

Among Iranians who came to the United States in 1979, 57 percent were professional, technical, or managerial workers. In Iran, only 6 percent of the workforce falls into those high-skill categories (Gibney 1990, 372). In that same year, 68 percent of the immigrants from India fell into these high-skill categories, compared to less than 5 percent among the entire Indian workforce (Gibney 1990, 372). Finally, 15 percent of the 6,000 Haitians who entered the United States in 1979 through normal immigration channels (as opposed to being refugees) were professionals, administrators, or managers, compared to 1 percent for the Haitian workforce (Gibney 1990, 372).

Even among refugees, however, there is evidence that skill and education levels are above the average of their compatriots. For example, Rita Simon

(1984b) shows that 48 percent of male Soviet Jewish refugees entering the United States in the 1960s and 1970s had been engineers in the Soviet Union. Of the first wave of late–1970s Vietnamese refugees—admittedly the most skilled and "easiest to settle" of the groups from that war-torn country—56 percent were in white-collar jobs in the United States by 1984, compared with less than 20 percent for all of Vietnam (Loescher and Scanlon 1986).

There is even evidence that illegal immigrants are not the poverty-stricken and least-skilled of their native countries. Surveys of undocumented immigrants to the United States from Mexico document that only about 5 percent of them were unemployed in Mexico, whereas the average Mexican unemployment rate was about three times that level. A much higher percentage of Mexican undocumented immigrants worked in white-collar occupations in Mexico than the average among Mexican citizens. And illiteracy among the undocumented Mexicans is about 10 percent, compared to about 22 percent for the Mexican population as a whole (Portes and Rumbaut 1990).

The Children of Immigrants

Perhaps the greatest and most overlooked contribution of immigrants to the economy is their progeny—including both those who come to the United States with their parents and those who are born in the United States of immigrant parents. The *Washington Post* (23 June 1990) highlighted the remarkable level of achievement of the children of immigrants:

> Thirteen of the 17 valedictorians in Boston public high schools this year are foreign-born, the highest number officials can remember.
>
> They come from around the world, including from China, Vietnam, Portugal, El Salvador, France, Italy, Jamaica, and Czechoslovakia. Some arrived only in the last five years, most could not speak English when they arrived. School officials attributed the high percentage to an influx of immigrants and the motivation of children who had to overcome tremendous obstacles just to get into the United States.

Public high schools in Washington, DC, Chicago, and Los Angeles also report remarkably disproportionate numbers of immigrant children as valedictorians. Another measure of the high level of achievement of immigrants is the number of Westinghouse Science Awards they win:

In 1988 the two highest honors in the national Westinghouse Science Talent Search went to immigrant students in New York public schools: Chetan Nayak from India and Janet Tseng from Taiwan. Since 1981 almost one-third of the scholarship winners in this high school competition, the oldest and most prestigious in the United States, have been Asian-Americans. *(Time,* 4 December 1988, 134)

The children of immigrants also tend to reach exceptionally high levels of achievement as adults, in terms of earnings and professional skills. The normal pattern has been that immigrants who enter as adults are often entrepreneurs or wage-earners who scrimp and save and work long hours to make a better life for their children; and they are successful at this. The children of immigrants tend to be overrepresented in highly paid professions, including medicine, law, and business management. Among almost all ethnic groups, earnings are higher among the children of immigrants than of the immigrants themselves (Chiswick 1979). Moreover, second-generation immigrants have more economic success than third- and fourth-generation Americans. Economist Barry Chiswick has calculated that throughout this century, the children of immigrants have had earnings that are on average 10 percent above those of comparably educated US–born children (cited in McConnell 1988, 101). This means that one cost of limiting immigrant admissions would be the loss of immigrants' talented and motivated children.

Immigration and US Economic Growth:
Past and Future

By the middle of the twentieth century, America surpassed all other nations in living standards and output. This economic growth coincided with several periods of very heavy immigration to the United States. Several studies have found that immigrants contributed directly to this economic expansion. The last stage of a study by Richard Vedder, Lowell Galloway, and myself investigated the impact of immigration on annual US economic growth rates from 1926 to 1987. Economic growth was measured as the amount of capital available to workers, or the capital-labor ratio, which is a critical determinant of wages and per capita output. The study (Vedder, Galloway, and Moore 1990) finds that the capital-labor ratio is positively associated with the percentage of foreign-born at any given time in a statistically significant sense.

Other studies on the overall economic impact of immigrants have come to similar conclusions. A comprehensive analysis of the effect of immigration on the nation's economic well-being by the President's Council of Economic Advisers (1986) concludes that "the net effect of an increase in the labor supply due to immigration is to increase the aggregate income of the native born population."

Interestingly, the positive impact of immigrants on the aggregate incomes of natives is true even of the lowest-skilled immigrants, despite the fact that they may lower wages for some workers. For example, the US Department of Labor (1989) finds: "Low skilled immigrants usually increase the average earnings of higher-skilled workers and the profits returned to capital. In fact, immigration increases aggregate income by more than the immigrants wages—regardless of his or her skill level" (p. 18; see also Chiswick 1979, 357–99).

The vast majority of economists agree with this benign assessment. In 1989 I surveyed the past presidents of the American Economic Association, the US winners of the Nobel prize in economics, and the past members of the President's Council of Economic Advisers for a study sponsored by the Hudson Institute and the Alexis De Tocqueville Institute (Moore 1990b). Of the forty respondents, 80 percent believed that immigration has had a "very positive impact" on US economic growth in the twentieth century. None of the respondents believed that the impact has been negative. Roughly two-thirds of these top economists believed that increased immigration would have a "favorable impact on the US standard of living."

There is near-universal agreement that immigration has had a positive economic impact in this century, but what about the next? How would we go about predicting which nations will grow rich and prosperous in the twenty-first century? And what factors will be most critical to a nation's economic growth?

In the past, scholars and political leaders have believed that those nations richest in natural resources, or which had the mightiest militaries, the strongest bodies, or the widest empires would prosper. In the next century, however, the comparative advantage will almost certainly belong to those nations with the most inventive minds and with economic systems that reward talented people to generate new products and new technologies that lead to the creation of new wealth. That is, in the next century, the scarcest natural resource will be talent and brainpower.

To retain its economic primacy in the world, the United States unquestionably must improve its education system and its training system for native-born Americans. But this should not, as some scholars suggest, preclude the adoption of a strategic immigration policy that exploits America's almost unique ability among nations to import needed human capital through the immigration process, which can be done at virtually no cost to American citizens. Indeed, the United States is already doing this today to a significant—though underappreciated—extent.

A liberal immigration policy is a critical step to ensuring that the twenty-first century, like the twentieth, is an American century.

References

Altonji, Joseph, and David Card. 1990. "The Effects of Immigration on the Labor Market Outcomes of Natives," in *Immigration, Trade, and the Labor Market,* edited by Richard B. Freeman and John M. Abowd. Chicago: University of Chicago Press.

American Engineering Association. 1990. Statement before the House Judiciary Committee, US Congress. Washington, DC (April).

Baker, Reginald, and David S. North. 1984. *The Vietnamese Refugees: Their First Five Years in America.* Washington, DC: New Trans Century Foundation.

Barkan, Elliott. 1989. "California at the Forefront: Pacific Rim Migration and Naturalization Patterns in the 1970s and 1980s," *ISSR Working Papers in the Social Sciences.* Los Angeles: University of California at Los Angeles, Institute for Social Science Research.

Bean, Frank D., Lindsay Lewis, and Lowell J. Taylor. 1988. "Undocumented Mexican Immigrants and the Earnings of Other Workers in the United States," *Demography* (February), 35–39.

Becker, Gary S. 1992. "The Migration of People," Remarks at the Annual Meeting of the Mont Pelerin Society, Vancouver, British Columbia, Canada.

Bogen, Elizabeth. 1986. Testimony before the Joint Economic Committee, US Congress. *Hearings on the Economic and Demographic Consequences of Immigration.* Washington, DC: US Government Printing Office (29 May).

8

150   STILL AN OPEN DOOR?

Borjas, George. 1990. *Friends or Strangers? The Impact of Immigration on the US Economy*. New York: Basic Books.

Briggs, Vernon M., Jr. 1992. *Mass Immigration and the National Interest*. Armonk, NY: M. E. Sharpe.

Brimelow, Peter. 1992. "Rethinking Immigration," *National Review* (18 April).

Buchanan, Patrick. 1990. "The Immigration Bomb," *Washington Times* (11 October).

Bureau of the Census. 1984. *Socioeconomic Characteristics of the US Foreign-Born Population Detailed in the Census Bureau Tabulations*, Release CB84-179. Washington, DC: US Department of Commerce.

Bureau of the Census. 1982. *Survey of Minority-Owned Business Enterprises, 1982—Blacks, Hispanics, and Asian Americans*, Release MB82-1/3. Washington, DC: US Department of Commerce.

Butcher, Kevin F., and David Card. 1991. "Immigration and Wages: Evidence from the 1980s," *American Economic Review* (May), 292–96.

Card, David. 1990. "The Impact of the Mariel Boatlift on the Miami Labor Market," *Industrial and Labor Relations Review* (January), 245–57.

Chiswick, Barry R. 1979. "The Economic Progress of Immigrants: Some Apparently Universal Patterns," in *Contemporary Economic Problems*, edited by William Fellner. Washington, DC: American Enterprise Institute.

———. 1978. "The Effect of Americanization on the Earnings of Foreign Born Males," *Journal of Political Economy* (October), 897–921.

Council of Economic Advisers. 1986. "The Economic Effects of Immigration," *Economic Report of the President, 1985*. Washington, DC: US Government Printing Office.

Council of Europe. 1986. *Recent Demographic Developments in the Member States of the Council of Europe*. Reprinted in Stephen Moore, "A Pro-Family, Pro-Growth Immigration Policy for America," *Backgrounder*. Washington, DC: Heritage Foundation, 1989.

DeFreitas, Gregory, and Adriana Marshall. 1984. "Immigration and Wage Growth in US Manufacturing in the 1970s," *Proceedings*, Annual Meeting of the Industrial Relations Research Association. Madison, WI: Industrial Relations Research Association, 148–56.

DeFreitas, Gregory. 1988. "Hispanic Immigration and Labor Market Segmentation," *Industrial Relations* 27, 195–214.

Duleep, Harriet Orcutt, and Mark C. Regets. 1992. "The Elusive Concept of Immigrant Quality," unpublished manuscript.

Dunn, William. 1990. "Asians Build New Lives as Immigrants," *USA Today* (26 November), A1.

Easterlin, Richard A. 1968. *Population, Labor Force, and Long Swings in Economic Growth*. Cambridge, MA: National Bureau for Economic Research.

Fallows, James. 1983. "Immigration: How It's Affecting Us," *Atlantic Monthly* (November).

Filer, Randolph K. 1988. "The Impact of Immigrant Arrivals on Migration Patterns of Native Workers," paper presented at the US Department of Labor Conference on Immigration, Washington, DC.

Forbes, Susan. 1985. *Adaptation and Integration of Recent Refugees to the United States*. Washington, DC: Refugee Policy Group.

Fossedal, Gregory A. 1990a. "Cry the Beloved Statue," Copley News Service.

———. 1990b. "Immigration Juggernaut," *San Francisco Chronicle* (28 March).

Francese, Peter. 1990. "Aging America Needs Foreign Blood," *Wall Street Journal* (27 March) (editorial).

Freeman, Richard B., and John M. Abowd. 1990. *Immigration, Trade, and the Labor Market*. Chicago: University of Chicago Press.

Funkhouser, Edward, and Stephen J. Trejo. 1993. "The Decline in Immigrant Labor Market Skills: Did It Continue in the 1980s?" unpublished manuscript. Santa Barbara: University of California.

Gibney, Mark. 1990. "United States Immigration Policy and the 'Huddled Masses' Myth," *Georgetown Immigration Law Journal* (Fall), 361–86.

Greenwood, Michael H., and G. L. Hunt. 1984. "Migration and Interregional Employment Redistribution in the United States," *American Economic Review* (December), 957–69.

Greenwood, Michael J., and J. M. McDowell. 1986. "The Labor Market Consequences of US Immigration: A Survey," *Journal of Economic Literature* (December), 1738–72.

Gurwitz, Aaron. 1991. *The Fiscal Outlook for New York City: A Longer View*. New York: Goldman Sachs.

Handlin, Oscar. 1951. *The Uprooted: The Epic Story of the Great Migrations that Made the American People*. Boston: Little, Brown.

Higham, John. 1963. *Strangers in the Land: Patterns of American Nativism, 1860–1925*. New Brunswick, NJ: Rutgers University Press.

Hof, Robert D. 1992. "High Tech's Huddled Masses: Making a Mark in Silicon Valley," *Business Week* (13 July).

Holden, Constance. 1989. "Debate Warming Up on Legal Migration Policy," *Science*.

Huddle, Donald C. 1982. "Undocumented Workers in Houston Non-Residential and Highway Construction: Local and National Implications of a Field Survey," unpublished manuscript. Houston: Rice University, Department of Economics.

James, Daniel. 1992. "Big Immigrant Wave Swamps Assimilation," *Wall Street Journal* (2 July), A9.

Johnston, William B., and Arnold Packer. 1987. *Workforce 2000*. Indianapolis: Hudson Institute.

Kirkpatrick, Jeane. 1986. "We Need the Immigrants," *Washington Post* (30 June), A11.

Kirwan, William E. 1990. Testimony before the Immigration Task Force, Subcommittee on Immigration, Refugees, and International Law of the House Committee on the Judiciary, US Congress. Washington, DC (1 March).

Kittredge, Frank D. 1989. Statement on behalf of the National Foreign Trade Council before the Subcommittee on Immigration and Refugee Affairs of the Senate Committee on the Judiciary, US Congress. Washington, DC (3 March).

Kotkin, Joel. 1992. *Tribes*. New York: Random House.

————. 1989. "America's Rising Sun," *Reason* (January).

LaLonde, Robert J., and Robert H. Topel. 1991. "Immigrants in the American Labor Market: Quality, Assimilation, and Distributional Effects," *American Economic Review* (May), 297–302.

Lamm, Richard. 1986. Testimony before the Joint Economic Committee, US Congress. Washington, DC (29 May).

Lamm, Richard D., and Gary Imhoff. 1986. *The Immigration Time Bomb: The Fragmenting of America*. Washington, DC: Federation for American Immigration Reform.

Lerner, J., and R. Roy. 1984. "Numbers, Origins, Economic Value and Quality of Technically Trained Immigrants into the United States," *Scientometrics* 6, 243–59.

Levinew, Richard. 1990. "Young Immigrant Wave Lifts New York Economy," *New York Times* (30 July).

Light, Ivan, and Angel A. Sanchez. 1987. "Immigrant Entrepreneurs in 272 SMSAs ," *Sociological Perspectives* (October), 373–99.

Loescher, G., and J. Scanlon. 1986. *Calculated Kindness: Refugees and America's Half-Open Door*. New York: Free Press.

Los Angeles County Board of Supervisors. 1992. *Impact of Immigrants on County Services*. Los Angeles, CA.

Mandel, Michael, and Christopher Farrell. 1992. "The Immigrants: How They're Helping to Revitalize the US Economy," *Business Week* (13 July).

McCarthy, Kevin, and R. Burciago Valdez. 1985. *Current and Future Effects of Mexican Immigration in California: Executive Summary*. Santa Monica, CA: RAND Corporation.

McConnell, Scott. 1988. "The New Battle over Immigration," *Fortune* (9 May).

Mines, R., and J. Avina. 1985. "Immigrants and Labor Standards: The Case of California Janitors," unpublished manuscript. Berkeley: University of California.

Moore, Stephen. 1993. "The Myth of America's Underfunded Cities," *Policy Analysis*. Washington, DC: Cato Institute.

——. 1991. "Mixed Blessings," *Across the Board* (March), 45–49.

——. 1990a. "Flee Market," *Policy Review* (Spring).

——. 1990b. *How Economists View Immigration*. Stanford, CA: Alexis de Tocqueville Institute; and Indianapolis: Hudson Institute.

——. 1990c. *People and American Competitiveness: Estimating the Economic Impact of Legal Immigration Reform*. Stanford, CA: Alexis de Tocqueville Institute.

——. 1989. "A Pro-Family, Pro-Growth Immigration Policy for America," *Backgrounder*. Washington, DC: Heritage Foundation.

Muller, Thomas, and Thomas J. Espenshade. 1985. *The Fourth Wave: California's Newest Immigrants*. Washington, DC: Urban Institute.

Myer, Michael. 1992. "Los Angeles 2010: A Latino Subcontinent," *Newsweek* (9 November).

National Research Council. 1988. *Foreign and Foreign-Born Engineers in the United States: Infusing Talent, Raising Issues*. Washington, DC: National Academy Press.

National Science Foundation. 1986. *Foreign Citizens in US Science and Engineering: History, Status, and Outlook,* special report, NSF 86–305. Washington, DC: National Science Foundation.

Office of Refugee Resettlement, US Department of Health and Human Services. 1989. *Refugee Resettlement Program*. Washington, DC: US Government Printing Office.

Papademetriou, Demetrious, and Thomas Muller. 1987. *Recent Immigration: Labor Market and Social Policy Issues*. Washington, DC: National Commission on Employment Policy.

Portes, Alejandro, and Robert L. Bach. 1985. *Latin Journey: Cuban and Mexican Immigrants in the United States.* Berkeley: University of California Press.

Portes, Alejandro, and Ruben G. Rumbaut. 1990. *Immigrant America.* Berkeley: University of California Press.

Rumbaut, Ruben G. 1991. *The Recentering of America: American Society in Transition.* Berkeley: University of California Press.

Seghal, Ellen. 1985. "Foreign Born in the US Labor Market: Results of a Special Survey," *Monthly Labor Review* (July), 18–24.

Simon, Julian, and Stephen Moore. 1989. "Communism, Capitalism and Economic Growth," *Backgrounder.* Washington, DC: Heritage Foundation.

Simon, Julian L. 1990. *The Economic Consequences of Immigration.* Cambridge, MA: Basil Blackwell.

———. 1984. "Immigrants, Taxes, and Welfare in the United States," *Population and Development Review* (March), 55–69.

———. 1981. *The Ultimate Resource.* Princeton, NJ: Princeton University Press.

Simon, Julian L., Stephen Moore, and Richard Sullivan. 1993. "The Effect of Immigration upon Unemployment: An Across City Estimation," *Journal of Labor Research.*

Simon, Rita J., and Julian L. Simon. 1984. "Social and Economic Adjustment," in *New Lives: The Adjustment of Soviet Jewish Immigrants in the United States and Israel,* edited by Rita J. Simon. Lexington, MA: Lexington Books.

Simon, Rita. 1984a. *American Opinion and the Immigrant.* Lexington, MA: Lexington Books.

Simon, Rita J., ed. 1984b. *New Lives: The Adjustment of Soviet Jewish Immigrants in the United States and Israel.* Lexington, MA: Lexington Books.

Social Security Administration. 1989. *Federal Old-Age and Survivors Insurance and Disability Insurance Trust Funds,* Board of Trustees Report. Washington, DC: SSA.

Sorenson, Elaine, and Maria E. Enchautegui. 1992. *Immigrant Male Earnings in the 1980s: Divergent Patterns by Race and Ethnicity.* Washington, DC: Urban Institute.

Sowell, Thomas. 1981. *Ethnic America.* New York: Basic Books.

Tepper, Elliot L. 1988. "Self-Employment in Canada among Immigrants of Difference Ethno-Cultural Backgrounds," *Employment and Immigration in Canada* (November).

Topel, Robert. 1990. "The Impact of Immigration on the Labor Market," in *Immigration, Trade, and the Labor Market,* edited by Richard B. Freeman and John M. Abowd. Chicago: University of Chicago Press.

Toth, Jennifer. 1991. "Study Will Spotlight Record of Success by Arab-Americans," *Los Angeles Times* (10 January), A5.

US Department of Labor, Bureau of International Labor Affairs. 1989. *The Effects of Immigration on the US Economy and Labor Market,* Immigration Policy and Research Report 1. Washington, DC: US Government Printing Office.

US General Accounting Office. 1988a. *Immigration: The Future Flow of Legal Immigration to the United States.* Washington, DC (January).

———. 1988b. *Sweatshops in the US: Opinions of Their Extent and Possible Enforcement Problems.* Washington, DC.

Ugalde, Antonio, Frank D. Bean, and Gilbert Cardenas. 1979. "International Migration from the Dominican Republic," *International Migration Review* (Summer), 235–54.

Vedder, Richard, Lowell Galloway, and Stephen Moore. 1990. "Do Immigrants Increase Unemployment or Reduce Economic Growth?" *Congressional Record* (26 September).

Wattenberg, Ben J. 1991. *The First Universal Nation.* New York: Macmillan.

———. 1985. *The Birth Dearth.* Washington, DC: American Enterprise Institute.

Williamson, Jeffrey. 1982. "Immigrant Inequality Trade-offs in the Promised Land: Income Distribution and Absorptive Capacity Prior to the Quotas," in *The Gateway: US Immigration Issues and Policies,* edited by Barry R. Chiswick. Washington, DC: American Enterprise Institute, 251–88.

Wong, Benjamin. 1988. *Patronage, Brokerage, Entrepreneurship, and the Chinese Community in New York.* New York: AMS Press.

Index

Abowd, John M., 123, 236
Africa: immigrants from, 14, 17
African Americans, 13-14, 15-16, 33,
    34, 49-54, 61, 64-65, 106, 143;
    effect of immigration on, 49,
    51-54, 103, 104, 110, 111, 129,
    130. *See also* Minorities; Slaves
Aging of US population, 12, 32,
    89-90. *See also* "Baby boom"
    generation
Agriculture, 59; immigrant
    employment in, 21, 26, 42, 44, 46,
    53, 79, 106, 121; role in US
    economy, 3, 12-13, 38, 39, 44, 121
Aid for Families with Dependent
    Children (AFDC), 91, 93, 133.
    See also Welfare assistance
Alexis de Tocqueville Institute, 89, 93,
    141, 146
Altonji, Joseph, 104
Amalgamated Clothing and Textile
    Workers Union, 107
American Economic Association, 146
American Engineering Association, 100
American Megatrends, Inc., 142

Americans with Disabilities Act of
    1990, 65
Anti-immigrant sentiments. *See* Public
    opinion toward immigration
Apparel industry. *See* Textiles and
    apparel
Applied Materials, Inc. 137
Arab immigrants, 120
Arkansas, 38
Artists: as immigrants, 7
Asian Americans, 5, 33-34, 40, 64
Asian immigrants, 128; admission
    levels of, 17, 19-20, 24, 27, 54,
    87-88, 119; relative success of, 88,
    97, 118, 119-20, 137, 142;
    restrictions on entry by, 14, 113,
    114; skills of, 80, 85, 119;
    Vietnam War and, x, 20
AST Research, 142
Asylees, 9, 10, 20-21, 24, 44, 47, 58,
    66-67
Asylum Officer Corps, 67
Attorney General, US, 20,59
Australia, 58, 84, 85
Avina, Jeffrey, 52, 104

Levinew, Richard, 131
Lewis, Lindsay, 111
Light, Ivan, 108
Literacy, 5, 60-61, 64, 143. *See also*
    Education; Skills of immigrants
Loescher, G., 144
Los Angeles, 51, 52, 78, 102, 103,
    107, 123, 125, 128-29, 140, 144;
    1992 riots in, 52, 53, 128
Los Angeles Country Board of
    Supervisors, 91-92
Lukasiewicz, John M., 38

Managerial and professional jobs, 38,
    39, 42, 79, 117, 120, 121, 143, 145
Mandel, Michael, 136, 140, 142
Manufacturing sector, 13, 35-38, 40,
    50, 104, 107n, 109-110, 111, 121,
    129
Mariel boatlift of Cuban refugees
    (1980), 130
Marshall, Adriana, 109
Marshall, Ray, 47
Mass immigration to the United States,
    3, 5, 8, 9-14, 19, 30, 34, 35, 44,
    49, 51, 54, 109, 124
Massachusetts, 102, 135
McCarthy, Kevin, 47, 94, 95, 120, 129
McConnell, Scott, 145
McCormack, Thelma, ix
McDonald, Gordon J., 124
McDowell, J. M., 100n
Medicaid, 91, 133. *See also* Welfare
    assistance
Medicare, 89, 90, 96
Mexico, 15, 18, 21, 78, 106;
    immigrants from, 94-95, 103, 107,
    111, 118, 120, 129, 131, 136, 140
Miami, 51, 102, 103, 123, 125, 128,
    129-31, 140.
Mid-Atlantic region, 38

Middle East: immigration from, 20
Midwest, 4, 40, 124
Miles, Jack, 52, 53
Military service, as disincentive for
    immigration, 15
Mines, Richard, 52, 53, 104
Mining, 13, 37
Minorities, employment of, 5, 8,
    15-16, 33, 34, 40, 51, 54, 57,
    64-65, 105. *See also* African
    Americans; Asian Americans;
    Hispanics
Mollica, Joseph, 136
Moore, Stephen, 82, 86, 87, 89, 97,
    98, 101, 102, 121, 124, 125, 126,
    127, 136, 145, 146
Mowry, David C., 40
Muller, Thomas, 47, 94, 95, 103, 107,
    128-29, 130
Myer, Michael, 94-95, 124

Napoleon Bonaparte, 12
National Academy of Sciences, 139;
    National Research Council of,
    46-47, 37, 138-39
National Origins Act. *See* Immigration
    Act of 1924
National origins system, 14, 16, 17,
    27. *See also* Immigration Act of
    1924
National Research Council. *See*
    National Academy of Sciences
National Science Foundation, 138
Native Americans, 34
"New" immigrants versus "old"
    immigrants, 19-22, 30, 44, 45-46,
    86-88, 113-22. *See also* Immigrants
New Jersey, 30, 46, 123
New Orleans, 40
New York (State of), 38, 46, 123